There were so many things in this book that related to me even though I had a totally different upbringing... Though I had no children of my own, this book was easy to relate to in so many ways. I also had a Granny (not directly related) who had a wonderful recipe for noodle pudding. I could not duplicate hers, but I created my own and passed it on to other family members who were unable to duplicate my formula even with a detailed recipe. I am looking forward to sending this book out to so many of my friends who need to hear this story.

— Irene Gold, R.N., B.S., M.A., D.C.
Founder, Irene Gold Associates and Chiropractic Board Review

Not Just For Moms...
As the father of 4 home-birthed, homeschooled, free spirit children of my own, I can tell you Dr. Patti's book is a breath of fresh air. It is unapologetically authentic and, well, just plain real. I remember after the birth of our first child, my wife turned to me and said, "I feel like everyone lied to me." This book doesn't lie to you. It's raw and it tells it to you like it is. Starting a family is crazy, challenging, and messy, and also transformational, empowering, and beautiful. I wouldn't have it any other way. Enjoy!

— Justin Ohm, DC
Executive Director, International Chiropractic Pediatric Association

Dr. Patti has written a must read for everyone. *Holy Sh*t! I'm Gonna Be a Mom! What Was I Thinking?* offers stories and pearls of wisdom that guide us to stay connected and feel blessed as a parent. Like a chef who knows her way around a kitchen, her "recipes" for being the best parents we can grow into are delightful and filled with love, kindness, and a huge heart. This is the book our children would want us to read, integrate, and then speak and act as if Dr. Patti were coaching us.

Whether you are a parent or not, we all love to interact with people who guide us with good intentions and a big heart. This life-changing book is meant for and dedicated to everyone who yearns to be the best parent they can be in their personal and professional lives.

— Barry Taylor, ND, *LOVE YOUR BODY: Your Path to Transformation, Health & Healing*

Dr. Patti is able to capture her readers with stories, humor, and emotion. This "recipe" is more than just for parenting; it is for all relationships. As she shares her parenting journey, we realize that parenting is a process of receiving and learning as much as it is one of raising and supporting.

— Dr. Peter Kevorkian, DC, FICPA, FCSC
Executive Vice-President for Institutional Advancement, Life Chiropractic College West

Dr. Patti's commitment to motherhood and her life's work has inspired countless others to open up their futures. She is a beacon of vitality. Her vision and dedication to healing have shaped the lives of many, creating a love a that embodies the true spirit of mothering through her unwavering dedication to wellness and health.

— Nancy Miriam Hawley
Founder and Co-Author, *Our Bodies, Ourselves*

The heartfelt and honest recollections and stories are a reflection of the author's steadfast belief that Mother-wisdom is a gift we must trust and use as we raise our families. From grandmother Sabaluche to Mother, to self and to children, Patti Giuliano shows us the wisest way is OUR way.

— Peg Doyle, M.Ed., Author of *Food Becomes You*

*Holy Sh*t! I'm Gonna Be a Mom! What Was I Thinking?* is SOOOO applicable to anyone!!! I found every story relatable. It's so lovely how Dr. Patti ties everything back to recipes and parenting. This is brilliant!

— Stephanie Libs, DC, Lactation Consultant

This book is a true feast for the soul—unconventional, wise, and so honest that it's refreshingly raw. Dr. Patti Giuliano serves up wisdom that nourishes the spirit and brings a tear to the eye. It's a must-have for parents at any stage, providing invaluable insights for raising all kinds of children. The book creates a vast, deep space for the parenting journey, allowing us to open our hearts wider and wider to embrace it all—the joy, the lessons, the messiness, and the love. [...This] book is nothing short of brilliant.

— Lisa Campion, *Awakening Your Psychic Ability*
Oracle, Psychic Mentor

Holy Sh*t!
I'm Gonna Be a Mom!

What Was I Thinking?

Dr. Patti Giuliano

with contributions by
Trisha J. Wooldridge

To my parents,
Cecelia Carola Giuliano and Armando Giuliano,
I salute you and all the other parents on the planet who
have had to wait for their children to have kids before
they are given the credit they deserve.
I love and appreciate you.

To my Grandmother, Isabella Carola (aka Sabaluche),
"Justa you watcha me," your recipe will live on!

To my children, Kathryn Elizabeth Giuliano Kevorkian
and Christopher Michael Giuliano Kevorkian,
this book would not be possible without you.
Thank you for being my greatest teachers.

To Dr. Peter Kevorkian,
my husband, the love of my life, and the most wonderful
dad on the planet. You inspire me to be my best self. Our
children and I would not be who we are without your
guidance and unconditional love. You are my "match
made in heaven." I love you forever!

Table of Contents

Foreword

Storyteller

"Justa you watcha me!"

\- Grandma Sabaluche

Many months before this book was published, I was getting antsy to see some kind of "product" from my labors. So my very smart and intuitive editor, Trisha, suggested I take a few chapters from the book and print up a mini preview to whet people's appetite.

For those of you who partook in the preview "antipasto", "Holy Sh#t! A Parenting Recipe. Justa You Watcha Me," *grazie* for your support and for being part of my "birthing team" for this, the entire book, *Holy Sh*t! I'm Gonna Be a Mom! What Was I Thinking?*

For those of you who are sitting down with these words for the first time, "Benvenuto e grazie!"

If you read my chap book and are wondering if you should skip ahead, hang in there a minute and let me tell you why you shouldn't.

I'm a storyteller. I have told these stories literally *hundreds* of times: at events, in workshops, for presentations, and during casual get-togethers. And just like how my recipes—to my husband's delight —are never *exactly* the same dish twice, my stories are never *exactly* the same with each telling.

To be honest, that's been one of the challenges in putting this project together. Each time I revisit a story, I'm in a different mental-emotional-physical place or I see a new need in my audience, so the story is altered just a little to have the greatest effect. (Hell, the day my editor sent my chap book to press, I called her with more changes!)

So what you're going to read in this book *will* be a little different than what you read in the chapbook. I couldn't help myself (and neither could my editor!). There are also a few more surprises—little interludes—such as where I've given my daughter, Katie, space to respond (as she requested in the prologue), additional "coffee break" stories that further illustrate the themes of each chapter, and even "side dishes" I invited my editor to bring to the table.

And consider this: As you read the entirety of this book, some things will resonate with *you* differently, regardless of any changes made on this end. So sit back and enjoy this entire meal with me—from the antipasto, to the dolci, and all the piatti in between—whether it's your first time at my table or one of many.

Side Dish from the (Editor) Sous Chef

*"So that's my wish for you, and all of us, and my wish for myself.
Make New Mistakes. Make glorious, amazing mistakes. Make
mistakes nobody's ever made before. Don't freeze, don't stop,
don't worry that it isn't good enough, or it isn't perfect, whatever
it is: art, or love, or work or family or life."*

- Neil Gaiman

Twenty-some-odd years ago, I sat down in a new chiropractor's office for my "welcome" intake appointment. It was a Saturday; I was wearing my favorite T-shirt with a sparkling Amy Brown faerie on it—something that totally wouldn't fly at my then-current financial job that (I naively expected) was a temporary position until I sold the Big Fat Fantasy book I was writing between calls that would totally kick off a best-selling, award-winning fantasy author career.

"Hi! I love your shirt. We should be friends!" A person-shaped ball of bright energy that looked somewhere between tween and teen sat next to me.

Having spent most of my life to that point as a precocious, awkward youth who struggled to make friends because she was effusively interested in weird stuff, I immediately recognized we were resonating on similar frequencies.

"Hi! Uh, okay, sure... Thank you! I'm Trish. What's your name?"

"I'm Katie. This is my parents' practice. This must be your first time..."

Dr. Patti, who was doing the intake appointments at that time, was running late, so Katie and I got to have a fantastic conversation that covered chiropractic, Dungeons & Dragons, writing, faeries, angels, hidden worlds, and probably a bunch more I don't remember.

It was the beginning of what still is a dynamic and (on more than one occasion) life-altering-for-the-better friendship.

After meeting Katie, I met Dr. Patti. From what I recall, we hit it off right away too, but one specific memory still stands out to me today.

I'd been asking what I needed to do, lifestyle-wise, exercise-wise to "fix" my spine. Or at least stop or reduce knocking it out of alignment, to stop or reduce my "subluxations" (the name for when a vertebra is out of alignment).

"You know what I've been wanting for years? I want a poster for this office that says 'Subluxations happen.' You know, like those posters that say 'Shit happens.'"

She went on to explain that all sorts of things will cause subluxations throughout our entire lives. The purpose of regular chiropractic adjustments wasn't to "fix" our backs, once and done, but to keep them aligned so that the body could function at its best ability.

To someone recently out of college, with loans, who came from a blue-collar family, looking to eventually have a career that would not provide any medical insurance beyond my husband's job benefits, the thought of paying for chiropractic care on top of any other doctor visits for the rest of my life was initially terrifying. But Patti, with her candid communication, gave off that same "we're vibrating on the same resonance" feel as her daughter.

Just as I was willing to explore a new friendship with Katie, I was willing to explore this new philosophy and

doctor-patient relationship with Patti.

My husband Scott (who has an uncanny amount in common with Dr. Peter) and I were regular patients at Westwood Family Chiropractic for only a few years before we moved to our current Worcester-area home, a little over an hour from Westwood, but our families remained friends.

Firstly, it helped that our new chiropractors, Drs. Jen and Rajeev Conners, were close friends to Patti and Peter—Dr. Peter was Dr. Raj's best man. Secondly, my friendship with Katie meant I was heading back to Westwood for things like D&D games, birthday parties, and graduations, as well as talks on wellness, fire walks, and more.

When Patti purchased her dream beach house, we helped them move in—down to Scott, Peter, and Christopher engineering the demolition and replacement of a fireplace wall that Scott still remembers fondly, and Patti sharing her amazing marinara recipe and onion pie with me. We attended several beach house parties and would occasionally rent it from Patti.

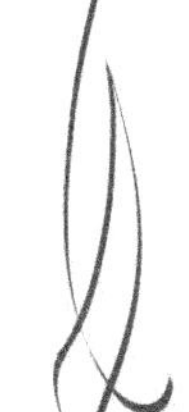

As I was finally getting into my publishing career, I started hosting creative retreats for my friends and colleagues at the beach house. Sometimes Patti joined us. About this time, she was starting to get serious about writing "her book." I would regularly give publishing feedback based on my experiences—and some fantastic failures—but I put up some boundaries.

And Patti very kindly respected those boundaries. Even when I would falter and say, "well, maybe I could...", she would outright ask what all I was doing at the time.

You see, like Patti, I have a tendency to Do All The Things. We're both also damn freaking good at things we're passionate about. *And* we also care deeply about helping people—often to the sacrifice of our own passions and dreams. Whenever Patti made me list everything I was working on—never less than three major projects with possibly three to five minor things—I would step back and say, "I honestly can't give your book the attention it deserves."

She would nod in knowing agreement. (Which, after

helping with this book, I can now giggle back, *knowingly*.)

In retrospect, there was more truth in that statement than either she or I realized.

In the years of hosting creative retreats at the beach house and becoming more *friends* with Patti—beyond doctor-patient, mom-of-friend friendship—I honed my writing, editing, and publishing abilities. I also went through a lot of serious health changes, got diagnosed with ADHD (which explained *so much* of my life!), and grew as a person.

As of the publication of this book, I've edited over four hundred titles. Mostly fiction—and mostly horror, science-fiction, and fantasy—but also non-fiction, memoirs, spiritual books, and a lot of food writing. Several of my authors have gone on to be best-sellers and award-winners. In working for various midsize, small, and independent publishers over the span of two decades, I've learned a lot about *publishing*—all the magic that goes into making someone's heart-spun words into a *book*.

I was finally at a place—with a fresh book deal after years recovering from a prior publishing burn—where I was taking down my "editor" shingle to focus on my *writing* projects when Patti hit a wall with her book. She'd fallen out of love with it, despairing the effort she'd put into this passion project. I offered—insisted—to look at the most recent manuscript version.

Patti's words spoke to me on a lot of levels. I needed tissues. I—someone who had accepted she likely couldn't have kids with surprising relief—related to so much of the message.

I also recognized the common issue many newer authors experience: their unique voice was lost in trying to make a "marketable book." The spark had died in all the "ought to," "should do," and "must do" editing conversations. This book was still burning in Patti's heart, but she didn't have the passion for all the other pieces of "making a book." (Which, to be honest, have changed significantly in the past ten years!)

To be clear, I'm not saying anything against any of the other editors or ghost writers. Patti learned a lot in the

process and a lot of strong work was put into creating the manuscripts I reviewed. But like I tell all of my potential clients or people who ask me about editing: Not every author and not every editor will work well together on every project.

In any case, I resonated with Patti's stories and the book she wanted to write. Between my eclectic publishing path, my unconventional wellness journey, and my particular neurospicy flavor, I *intuitively* knew I had the skillset to not only help Patti achieve her dream but to rekindle her passion. Her book's message on parenting, its recipe, aligned with *my personal life philosophy*. I *love* the love she brings to the world with this book (and so much of the work she does), I love how she puts so much time and effort to helping others realize their best lives and dreams, and I love that I can help her achieve her dream and passion project.

(If you read the chap book, see what I did there?)

Lastly, as you start this book, you'll discover Patti is perfectly unconventional. And damn proud of it! (As she should be!) *Holy Sh*t! I'm Gonna Be a Mom!* is an equally unconventional parenting book. Authors get told "write the book you want to read," and that's what I wanted to help Patti do. Besides the traditionally numbered chapters, this book includes several "Coffee Break" and "Side Dish" sections, which more specifically explain certain points or offer different viewpoints (like that of her daughter or her editor). It's a lot like a family dinner full of related stories that, altogether, make a family narrative.

But to *really* understand, you need some of the digressions between the stories.

While I recommend reading this beginning to end for the fullest effect, Patti (and I) specifically wanted a book where people get a story and a message from any section they opened. We wanted it easy to bookmark, served in accessible and digestible portions you could revisit as needed for a pick-me-up or comfort snack or even a quick lunch date. We've also included notes, references, and resources to help you "customize" Patti's recipe to your family's needs and tastes.

I haven't a drop of Italian blood in me, but I'm just as

quick as Patti to mix up an impromptu meal for friends and family—or step in as sous chef for a host—so pull up a chair to Patti's table and join us! To quote Julia Child, another brilliant woman of cooking who inspired me, *Bon appétit!*

Prologue

Mother-Daughter Conversations

*"The relationship between parents and children, but especially
between mothers and daughters, is tremendously powerful,
scarcely to be comprehended in any rational way."*

- Joyce Carol Oates

After over twenty years working on this parenting book that lived in my heart, I was—and still am—terrified.

These stories reveal intimate details about not only my life, but that of my own parents, my husband, my kids, and other family members. I was (and still am) scared about how people who don't know me would judge us, and I worried certain family members might be offended by what I share.

Finally, just as I was in the final editing stages, I gathered enough courage to ask my then-thirty-six-year-old, neurospicy daughter, Katie, if she wanted to read the book before I published it.

I approached her in the laundry room, face to face in what I hoped to be a contained and friendly environment. The conversation went something like this: "Katie, I am almost done with the book. When I am done, will you read it and let me know if there is anything in there that would upset you?"

To which she replied, a little snarkily, I might add, "Well, Mom, if you are asking me that, you must think there is something I am going to be upset about!"

I had gone down a rabbit hole I might not be able to get out of. Looking for an escape, I said, "Never mind. It will all be okay."

Katie wasn't ready to end the conversation. She said she would like to read it and add her comments in the margins of the book so people would see her perspective about what I had written.

Oh shit! Where to go from there? "Well, my editor likely won't allow that."

"Oh really, Mom? It's your book, and you get to decide."

"Yes, you're right, Katie, but I don't think it is the best thing..." I tried to end the conversation again. "I'm sorry I even brought it up—"

"I don't give you permission to talk about me in the book at all!"

Holy Shit! I would have to edit out half of the book! Angry at myself for even starting the conversation, I said, "I don't want to talk about this," and left the room. I was ready to throw up.

Ten minutes later, I realized we had an unresolved situation and I didn't want to let it hang there.

The life of my book was at stake.

Katie was still in the laundry room, where we'd had many other wonderful conversations folding clothes and sheets. We would resolve this amicably. Or one of us might not make it out alive. Kidding makes things better, right?

Knowing I needed to take the high road, I apologized for upsetting Katie and explained the book had been a challenge to write because it reveals a lot about our family. "I'm worried about what I'm writing about my mother, too."

Katie had moved on from our original conversation and addressed my more recent actions. "Did your mom used to leave conversations on you like you just did to me?"

Holy shit! It hit me like a ton of bricks. Tears welled up in my eyes. "You're right."

She smiled, tears in her eyes, too.

"Every time my mother was upset, she'd get the car keys and storm out of the house. It scared the crap out of me, and I'd be so afraid she wouldn't come back home... Katie, you just helped me see that I have behaviors that I do unconsciously that I learned from my mother."

I had spent my whole life wanting to be somebody different from my mother. I wanted to parent differently, build a different relationship with my daughter than my mother had with me, and here I was, called out for being the person I most wanted not to be.

Still crying, I said, "Katie, thank you for being honest with me and having me see that I am just like my mother in many ways. And that's not such a bad thing. And I wish I had been a daughter more like you. You have always been my greatest teacher and you have insights that make me stop in my tracks and open my eyes to things about myself that I could improve upon."

We shared a sniffling hug.

Then I said, "I have to go write this down so I can use it in my book!" We laughed as I ran out of the laundry room. I could tell she was beaming for the contribution she had just made to me and the book.

Every generation wants their kids to have a better life than they did. And they cockily say they are going to do it better than their parents.

I have a sign in my house that says, "By the time a woman realizes her mother was right, she has a daughter who thinks she is wrong." I used to think it was funny, and now, I think it is sad that we stereotype mother-daughter relationships like that. We don't have to throw our parents under the bus, and we can't blame them for all our mishaps and challenges. And we can learn so much from our children if we put our egos aside and listen to them.

After all, many of their actions and responses were instilled in them by us.

Duh!

Just like every generation before and probably for generations to come.

Chapter One

The Blue Dot: The First Holy Shit! *of Many*

"Life is a journey, not a destination."
- Rev. Lynn H. Hough

"Holy shit! I'm gonna be a mom."

Before we get to becoming a mom, let's talk about *Holy shit!* And I don't mean diapers, though you'll get plenty of that too. But think about what is happening when we say "Holy shit!" That's something, right?

After spending what I remember to be hundreds of dollars on home pregnancy tests, the arduous task of peeing into a teeny tiny tube (try that sometime!), sticking a Q-Tip-sized white stick into the tube, and waiting for an eternity stuffed into ten minutes, I did not fully appreciate the *Holy shit!* aspect of that moment.

I had never seen the blue dot, and I wasn't sure I even believed what I saw! I hadn't thought about how I'd react in this moment. "Holy Shit!" was all I could think.

My life was about to change. My *understanding* of life was about to change.

Mind you, this certainly wasn't the first *Holy shit!* utterance or moment in my life, just the first in regard to parenting. The first of many. *Very* many.

And it wasn't until many Holy shit! moments had passed that I figured out those two little words signaled an important learning experience: an epiphany, if you will. And let me tell you, some lessons require more than a few Holy shit! moments to hit home. You'll see.

Now, back to the test.

Curiously, my husband, Peter, had been complaining about nausea for the past week and had suggested I test again.

I had all but given up on getting pregnant. We'd even started having discussions about adopting. So, his suggestion did not make me a happy camper!

Throw another $25 out the window? I was done!

But there was something to Peter's "symptoms;" my husband never gets nauseous. He even joked, "If I didn't know better, I'd say I was feeling pregnant."

I was cautiously curious. It may sound weird to some people, but I trusted what he was sensing and feeling. So I took the damn test.

And there was a blue dot.

After three and a half long years of trying to get pregnant, three and a half years of waiting to have a child we wanted so badly, three and a half years of exploring all possible means and "positions" (I'll save you the details ;-)), three and a half years of trying to freakin' convince my eggs to like my husband's sperm...

I stood alone in my bedroom with that amazing, magnificent, radiant blue dot staring up at me. I wanted to shout it to everyone!

Of course, I needed to let Peter know first. He was going to be a dad! And he needed to know that he'd been right. He'd felt the pregnancy before I had!

It wouldn't be the last time that Peter's intuition led to a discovery in our parenting career—but that's a later story.

Shit, I would have to wait to tell him. He was downstairs in the office, taking care of patients.

Damn! How could I wait? When I couldn't contain it any longer, I ran downstairs (a bit worried he might faint or possibly cry in front of his poor patient), and barged right in.

"You were right! I took the test! I'm pregnant!"

The room went silent.

Peter hugged me. And then we both cried. (And so did our patient).

But as Peter hugged me, all I could think was, *He knew!* And then, *I'm not at ALL prepared for this.*

The blue dot moment was so surreal. I thought I was emotionally prepared. Yes, I was excited. I mean, *really* excited. Peter was head over heels! But, oh my God! So many feelings. Disbelief, after so many disappointments. Then joy, excitement, and overwhelm.

The nerves quickly took over: *Oh my God, what do I do now? Am I ready? I should be.*

But *was* I? Really, *really* ready? I reached for a glass of wine. But oh no! I'm pregnant. I'll have to wait eight more months for that! Damn!

It was the mid-80s. We didn't have the internet. No Facebook. No YouTube. No Instagram. No TikTok. It wasn't like today, where at the click of a mouse, you are bombarded with thousands of data bits about anything and everything you could ever want to know about parenting, from how to get pregnant to what destination your kids will choose for their wedding.

Peter and I had spent those three and half years reading every book we could get our hands on, talking to every parent we knew, and watching every video we could find. We took in anything and did everything possible to get ready to be parents.

I knew deep down inside that we were going to do it "our way," and it would be perfect.

But with that blue dot, all that wonderful data flew out the window. I thought, *I am going to have to trust myself. I will know what to do.* I turned out pretty good, and I don't think my mother or grandmother or my grandmother's mother ever opened a book to learn how to be a good mother. I had the answers inside me. I would be a great *Mom*.

Or would I? My first big test would be getting through the next eight months of pregnancy, and then birthing this little being inside me.

Let's fast forward to the birth since the entire story will be revealed in a future chapter.

I had everything in place for my perfectly planned home birth: countless hours of research, loads of data, a birthing tub (okay, a repurposed horse trough), a midwife and birthing team, emergency services on call, and even ice cream to celebrate with afterwards.

And in a few minutes, all my plans for the perfect birth went to shit.

Kathryn Elizabeth Giuliano Kevorkian was born on May 5, 1987 —only ninety minutes after my water broke! I almost birthed her in the toilet. She wasn't breathing right away. And her Apgar score was just 2 out of 10.[1]

Despite all my research and planning, my perfect new baby hadn't tolerated the birthing process well and would need help adjusting outside of my womb.

Holy shit!

This almost seven-pound spirit was in control, and I could do nothing but pray she would make it!

***

The only time people are utterly certain they know everything about the world of parenting—conception, pregnancy and birth—is *before* they have kids! Isn't that the truth?

Even after traveling this road for years, I'm certain every parent has at least one moment of wondering if they are doing this whole thing entirely wrong—or worse, raising a psychopath.

If anyone tells you differently, I would bet they are lying or blissfully oblivious.

I thought I had all the answers, and then I faced the imminent reality of the needs, wants, and challenges of an impending birth.

Holy Shit! You can't know what you don't know until you know it! You know?

Hang in there. Don't let me scare you. There are perks to this experience. I promise.

Through all the craziness that may ensue, you can and will weather this parenting journey in a way that is deeply empowered, truly inspired, aligned with who you are as a person, and lets you and your child emerge ready to soar.

Or you may move to an island somewhere and not leave a forwarding address.

Seriously, I don't have all the answers when it comes to parenting. Far from it. No one does.

But I have discovered myself on a deeper level, stepped into greater personal growth and empowerment, and dealt with demons that I didn't even know I had before holding my newborn in my arms. I navigated my parenting journey by listening to my intuition, trusting myself and my philosophy, and surrendering to unconditional love—in its many facets. That freed me to embrace and forgive my very human shortcomings. It hasn't been without challenges, and I haven't always loved the hard parts.

In return, my children taught me more about myself than I ever could have imagined, and I embrace the blessings they have given me.

And surprisingly, in the most difficult but fruitful times, I've found a successful parenting journey lies in something simple—*profound*, yet simple.

And trust me, I need simple!

A simple recipe, you could say. The best kind of recipe—the kind you can adapt to your family's needs and tastes.

But like figuring out any other recipe, it's going to take a few "Holy Shit!" moments.

Coffee Break

On Pregnancy

"A universal intelligence is in all matter and continually gives to it all its properties and actions, thus maintaining it in existence."

- R. W. Stephenson, DC

As you get to know me through this book, you'll learn I look at things a little differently than a lot of people. When I need to make sense of something, I run it through my philosophy filter: How does this make sense based on how I look at the world as a "vitalist"?

What's a "vitalist," you ask? I'm glad you did!

A "vitalist" is someone who believes that life is intelligent. The Creator of our amazing bodies engineered them with inherent wisdom and genius so these bodies could naturally heal and adapt to the world in which they lived and functioned. So when it came to growing a new life inside my awesome body, I trusted everything I was feeling and experiencing was part of a divine design that would prepare me for when this baby would live outside of my body.

Both my pregnancies started with three and a half months of vomiting. Not fun! Especially since I had to recover from each vomiting episode and continue to see my patients.

Those kids started early to annoy the heck out of me! I wonder if that's why they used to hold babies upside-down and hit their bums when they were born. Ha! I'd be lying if I didn't say that thought crossed my mind.

But adhering to the belief in the wisdom of my body, trusting that everything that was happening for a reason, I went on a quest to understand the significance of that nausea. In my research, I found that nausea can be caused by an abundance of specific hormones related to the pregnancy (that not everyone will experience). Statistically, those abundant hormones that cause the nausea usually lead to an easier rest of the pregnancy, labor, and delivery.

For me, after I endured those three-plus months, everything else would be a piece of cake. Yay!

Whether it was mind over matter or not, after those first one hundred and five days, I was in a state of bliss, loving almost every minute of pregnancy. I was able to play racquetball to the end of my eighth month and continued to adjust patients until the day before I gave birth. Labor for my first baby, Katie, only lasted about ninety minutes. For Christopher, my second child, I was in labor for forty-three minutes. Something was definitely working in my favor!

Then there was getting up at night and peeing every two hours during pregnancy. How could this be perceived as wisdom? It prepares us for when a baby is born. They may need to nurse every two hours! That's a smart body!

And there was another biggie I learned: If I didn't eat as soon as I woke up or as soon I felt hungry, I would get nauseous and *hangry*.

What do babies do when they are hungry? They cry! And it is a different kind of cry than when they need a diaper change. It is a *hangry* cry. And you better get your boob or a bottle in that baby before they puke—or hold their breath, turn blue, and then let out a blood-curdling scream. (Not that I'd know from just such an experience...)

My philosophy—philosophy being one of the three ingredients in this book's parenting recipe!—can be expressed in a succinct way: *Everything the body does can be*

explained by understanding its physiology and by acknowledging there is a wisdom and genius in control. A good thing, because if pregnant people had to get up every morning and tell our future babies how to grow body parts in utero during their gestational period, humanity would not exist! There is a plan and an innate drive to survive and adapt within all living things, and when someone is growing a baby, *holy shit,* that is one of the biggest miracles I have ever seen the body do!

Chapter Two

A Recipe for Parenting: My Version

"This is my invariable advice to people: Learn how to cook—try new recipes, learn from your mistakes, be fearless and above all have fun."

- Julia Child, *My Life in France*

For most of us, our parenting strategies and philosophy are rooted in our childhood, how our parents raised us. It's so deeply programmed that I have said things to my kids that my parents said to me—that I vowed I would never say! Haven't you?

Who we become as people, as parents (or parents-to-be), comes down to a choice. That choice requires awareness that certain behaviors and beliefs learned from parents and other caregivers may or may not ring true to who we are. Then it takes a concentrated effort to adopt or reject those behaviors as we figure out who *we* are and how *we* want to show up in this world.

The bottom line is no matter how you perceive your upbringing or how you currently define and present yourself, your parenting choices are something you can prepare for.

I was born into a traditional Italian family in beautiful, picturesque...New Jersey.

Yeah, I'm a Jersey girl through and through. Need I say more?

Parenting was a group effort in my family. We lived in a three-story house on a cobblestone street. My parents, my siblings, and I lived on the first floor; my father's parents lived on the second; my aunt, uncle, and five cousins (also on my father's side) were on the third. We ate together; we played together. Looking back, it was kind of like being raised by the mob, minus the super illegal and extremely violent part.

A ton more relatives lived within two blocks of us, and my mother regularly shipped us off to different families. Probably to have some peace and quiet.

I was typically sent across the street, where my mother's parents (the Carolas) and my mother's brother, Uncle Louie, lived. My grandmother took care of me while Grandpa and Uncle Louie went off to work. A feisty 4'6", 200-pound Neapolitan, Isabella Carola *was* the "Original Gangster" who ruled the family—and the entire street!—with her expressive hand and mouth. So long as she wasn't within earshot, people called her "Sabaluche." (For the non-Italians, "Sabel," was short for "Isabella," and "uche" is a pet name meaning "the smaller or younger version of someone with the same name.") Should my grandmother overhear you calling her Sabaluche, she'd fire back "Fongul, you sonnamabeech," or she'd send you the evil eye.

Some of my fondest childhood moments were spent with Sabaluche, always wearing her apron-covered housedress, in the kitchen. She allowed me to join her for her three o'clock black coffee and anisette siesta, which was usually accompanied by biscotti or some other Italian cookie. Yes, she did put a few drops of anisette in my coffee too and told me "don-a you tell-a you muhther."

My mom, at age ninety-six, still has her coffee with Sambuca (*her* version of coffee siesta) every day at three o'clock, and in turn, my brother, my two sisters, me—and anyone with my mom at 3:00—carries on this tradition. I'm not even a coffee drinker, but it is almost sacrilegious not to join her.

As Grandma took this sacred coffee break, we would sit and talk. Or I should say, she would talk and I would listen. She told stories about her life in Italy, gossiped about the neighbors, or badmouthed certain relatives.

I wanted to grasp every word she said, but she would speak to me in half-English, half-Italian sentences. I was on the edge of my chair, anticipating the next word of the next story, so I'd interrupt to remind her to speak English.

When I did, she'd swear at me and say, "Whaddaya, stupida? I am-a speaka dee Ingalish. Justa you listen!"

I laugh now as I remember this. I was so frustrated, yet I never got offended. I wanted to stay on her good side, so she would keep talking.

Some of our other best bonding moments would be in the TV room, where we shared what every Italian grandmother and granddaughter cherished in their idle moments: World Heavyweight Wrestling. (That's what all grandmothers and granddaughters do, right?). I'd laugh to myself as she sat by me on the couch, swearing and screaming, "Fongul, you sonnamabeech!" while wildly gesturing at the TV and cheering on her favorite—Haystacks Calhoun—as he overpowered Bobo Brazil and Killer Kowalski, utterly convinced the fight was real.

Sabaluche was not someone who shied away from emotion. She was a strong, stubborn woman who didn't take shit from anyone, did not hold back her emotions, and I loved it!

It should come as no surprise our relationship was not the warm, fuzzy "hugs and Hallmark moments" others may have had with their grandmothers. She was a tough cookie: we only did what *she* wanted to do. I followed along without a thought that I might have a choice. Through all her emotional outbursts and her demanding personality, it was always special to be with her.

I especially *loved* it when we made homemade pasta—or should I say, she made it and I was allowed to assist. My favorite was making cavatelli (pronounced Gavadeel by New Jersey Italians): kneading the dough, rolling it out, cutting and shaping into tiny little boat-like pieces. We would place the finished pieces on a white cloth covered with semolina flour that draped over the porcelain table. It took hours. Every now and then, when she wasn't looking, I would sneak some raw dough into my mouth to taste. It was almost as good as the cooked version.

It was, and still is today, my favorite pasta.

I idolized Sabaluche more than any other relative, including my parents. I watched and learned and wanted to be like her: bold, courageous, and immune to what others thought about her.

Ten-year-old Patti had no idea Sabaluche's wisdom and ways would help her to discover who she wanted to be as a parent.

It wasn't any particular advice she gave, words she spoke, or anything written down. Her wisdom came in who she was, what she did, and how she responded to life.

The most profound lesson came when I finally got the courage to ask for her famed Gavadeel recipe. I will never forget that day.

She swore under her breath in Italian, trying to contain herself, before exclaiming, "Whaddaya, stupida? Justa you watcha me!"

I had been watching her for years, so I guess I should have known? In any case, I was so used to her—and most Italians—talking loudly, swearing, and being expressive that I didn't even flinch.

Little did I know I was about to learn one of the most valuable lessons that any of us can learn in life.

According to Sabaluche, if I wanted to make the Gavadeel, I had to learn what felt right, what smelled right, what tasted right, and what looked right. She taught me (or should I say, forced me to see) that good cooks tuned into intuition and followed traditions that were passed down through the generations.

So I "justa watcha" as she bade. Even though I had seen her work hundreds of times, this time I watched with an intensity unlike any other. I wanted to get it right and never forget again!

Countless times she reached into the giant twelve-by-eight-inch round, red and yellow aluminum tin (a repurposed old cookie tin) to spread flour on the four by four "macaroni" board (similar to a cutting board but bigger and handmade by my grandfather). Then she would pour salt into her palm and melt it into water, to which she next added eggs. She made a center bowl in the mound of flour and poured the beaten eggs and salt water (which I'd been allowed to beat under her strict supervision) into the center. Her hands slowly scooped around the inside of the flour bowl like a sculptor to draw in the liquid egg mixture.

"Grandma, can I do some?"

"No, you justa watcha me!"

I could have cried; I wanted to get my hands in there so badly. But I waited.

Once the flour and liquid were combined, she tasted the dough, made a face of disgust, and then added a little more salted water. Then she added a little more flour until she felt it was "justa right."

It was a beautiful sight. I was watching an artist.

About the time she started kneading the dough, she reached her limit and needed to sit down and rest.

I had my chance! "Grandma, can I do some?"

"Sí, sí," she said, catching her breath "But make-a sure you-a do it-a right. I'm-a watcha you."

I hoped and prayed I would do it right.

I dug my hands into the cool mixture and pushed it into itself, folding the ends over toward the middle, the bottom over the top, all while pressing it into the board to make it smoother and more pliable. The smell of fresh dough on my fingers was better than perfume. I didn't want to stop. But all things come to an end.

Sabaluche got up, pushed her finger into the dough, and announced that it was done!

My hands and arms felt like they were going to fall off, but I would never tell her that.

We let our perfectly rounded masterpiece sit for thirty minutes (timed perfectly with three o'clock coffee). After that, we began the transformation of rolling the kneaded mound into long tubes, cutting them into quarter-inch pieces, and rolling the dough under our fingers.

I was in Heaven. I was making Gavadeel with my grandma.

Over the years, there were many cooking experiences with Sabaluche, each one a story unto itself. But the essence of what and how she cooked (or did anything else in her life) was an artistic endeavor. Her acts expressed her love for her family. There was a method in the way Sabaluche brought together the elements and created dishes like no other (even to this day). And her food was the best! She told you so, just in case you might think anyone (especially our other grandmother) could even compete.

Knowing her style, understanding it, and then trusting my senses would make me a good cook like Sabaluche. From her, I would craft a "justa right" recipe for life and parenting.

***

Nowadays, we can search the internet for any recipe we want. Google a recipe for cavatelli, and you might get almost two million results, some wildly different and many not a good fit for your needs and kitchen capability.

Looking for parenting advice? You'll also get an overwhelming amount of information, much of it wildly different. And not necessarily the best for the masterpiece/child you are creating.

As a parent, I wanted to be a great cook and show my love for my family by crafting magnificent meals. But more than that, I wanted to have a positive influence on my kids, showing my love by being the best I could be at anything I did for them.

That was a high bar to sustain, as I would eventually realize.

Fortunately, I had the wisdom of Sabaluche's Gavadeel to guide me. And ground me.

"Whaddaya, stupida? Justa you watcha me!"

A few simple ingredients worked into a few simple steps became profound in the lack of exact measurements or rules so "justa right" could be attained no matter if the air was humid or dry, if the ingredients were fresh or about to turn sour, if the cook accomplished the task all at once or needed to take a break or three—or if the cook was a completely different person with her own personality and view of the world.

I would use my senses to combine the ingredients and adapt the recipe to who I was. I would cook for my family in a way that honored who they were, their unique physical needs and desires. Does that make me a pushover (as some would say)? No, it is who I am and how I want to show love to my family.

I'm talking about both the pasta and parenting, of course.

Sabaluche's Gavadeel recipe was exactly what I needed. Simple and profound.

But most of all simple. Like I said before, I need simple!

So here it is. Here's the recipe I share with you as my grandmother shared her Gavadeel recipe with me. (With perhaps a bit less swearing.)

Ingredients:	**Steps:**
Intuition Philosophy Unconditional Love	1. Trust your intuition. 2. Live true to your philosophy and beliefs. 3. Choose to love unconditionally.

You don't even have to perform these steps in a particular order. In fact, feel free to use them in whatever order best suits what will nourish your soul at any moment.

My desire in sharing this simple recipe for parenting is not to have you parent my way, but to have you take the basics, and then adapt and modify it to who you are and who your children are. The recipe is so simple that it is often bypassed by some who think we have to follow all the books or do what our friends are doing.

I say (a bit gentler than Sabaluche would), "Stop it! Justa be-a youself."

Be yourself, and adapt your parenting to each of your kids individually. Because each kid is an individual.

Simple ingredients worked into simple steps. Profoundly. Follow your philosophy and beliefs like Sabaluche followed the cooking traditions passed from the generations before her. Trust your intuition and your senses, like Sabaluche trusted whether she put enough salt into the mixture. Lastly—and most importantly—look at the experience as a way to share your love, as Sabaluche loved her family through the medium of food.

As parents, we can forget to act out of love sometimes. The more we act out of unconditional love, the better the outcome. That goes for the pasta or the experience with your child.

To this day, no matter how much I try, my kids will still say that Grandma's pasta is the best! I have found it impossible to recreate those famous dishes. Was it the water? Was it the type of flour? Was it some "secret" ingredient? I followed her basic Gavadeel recipe for years and just could not replicate it.

Then one day I changed it.

I am giving you trade secrets, so listen carefully.

First, I found Caputo double-zero flour, imported from Italy, which, while not technically gluten free, my gluten-free friends and I can eat without a problem. Had Grandma used this flour and not told me?

Next, I discovered sage-butter sauce from a gnocchi recipe given to me by my sister. *That* was a "Holy shit!" moment for me. Where had this sauce been all my life? No one in our family (not even extended family) had ever introduced us to that recipe.

You see, Sabaluche always made her Gavadeel with marinara sauce, and people loved it. The tomatoes, however, started to give me heartburn as an adult. My body changed, and that special dish that signified our cherished bond and that important lesson was now hurting my body! Realizing I could change it, that I could create it the way I needed it, preserved my favorite dish and all the love, lessons, and wisdom each bite carried.

I make my Gavadeel with double-zero flour and a sage-butter sauce, and my family loves it. Both Sabaluche's version and mine are amazing creations, and if she were alive today, I would jokingly tell her mine was best.

And then I would run!

But they both work.

As a parent, you get to create your own masterpieces: your children. You don't have to do it like me (or Sabaluche) or anyone else. The recipe I share uses ingredients already inside of you; the steps are ones you've been honing your entire life—consciously or subconsciously.

You're not-a stupida, but join me at my macaroni board. You've seen and done these steps possibly a hundred times before, but have you watched as intently as a ten-year-old watches her idolized grandmother make her family's most beloved food?

Justa you watcha me!

Chapter Three

Intuition: A Flash of Insight

"Intuition doesn't tell you what you want to hear; it tells you what you need to hear."

- Sonia Choquette

Have you ever had a moment when it all becomes clear? When the truth seems suddenly and abundantly apparent? Out of nowhere, a flash of insight reveals some deep, divine knowing?

For some, these moments are as rare as unicorns, and for others, they're so common as to be passé.

I can't tell you the exact moment when intuition first changed my direction, nor can I count how many of these moments have occurred in my life as a parent. But, one moment stands out in my mind as one of the riskiest choices I ever made. And it completely changed the course of my life.

It was a cold February day in 1983. I was at the Hynes Auditorium in the Back Bay of Boston, picking up after a group of chiropractors I'd shared a booth with at the New England Health and Lifestyle Expo. The people *actually* responsible for doing this job? Mysteriously MIA. My mother, who'd come to help like a good Italian Mama from New Jersey, hit the roof when I told her we needed to pack up the entire booth and carry all its contents to my apartment.

We Giuliano girls aren't the type to let things go half-done, so my mom and I cleaned everything up. All the while, my mother was swearing in Italian, demanding I hold the left-behind literature boxes and chiropractic equipment for ransom.

"Whatever you say, Mom." I rolled my eyes as I kept packing and she kept swearing. Haven't daughters been rolling their eyes at their moms for generations? No matter how old they are?

At a local professional gathering a few weeks later, I found the person responsible for my mother's outrage: Peter Kevorkian, a tall, dark-haired, dark-eyed chiropractor who had shown up at this business-casual meeting in a three-piece suit. Just like he had at the health fair.

I walked my cowgirl boot-wearing, hippie self right up to him and announced, "My mother said if you want your shit back, you have to buy me lunch."

Seeming to ignore the undisguised annoyance in my demand, he just smiled a slow smile and agreed. His voice was mesmerizing, like a sexy radio announcer.

But that was irrelevant because I was unavailable. Sort of. I had a fiancé back in Atlanta, but I was about to put my engagement and subsequent wedding on hold.

I loved my fiancé; we'd shared seven years of life together. But he wouldn't hold my hand or show any affection in public. He inspired an urge in me to help and heal him, but managed to make me feel needy, drained, and small.

Still, I called on my Jersey Girl mask of bravado, and it didn't fail. "Well, it's going to have to be next week, because I'm going back to Atlanta to see my honey."

Again, that slow smile. "Yes, that's fine. I'll look forward to it."

I was shocked to find myself making good on my promise to my mother.

When that lunch date arrived on April 1st, Peter and I sat in the Seventh Inn café on Newbury Street and talked easily about life, the universe, our philosophies, and our lives as chiropractors. Our minds met so effortlessly.

Apparently, however, I had talked non-stop about my Atlanta fiancé who'd encouraged me to go to chiropractic school, lived with me, and supported me on all levels while I completed my degree. Even now, I'm sure Jerry had loved me in the best way he knew how.

But I was living in a state of denial and delusion. In my mind, I was working out the logistics of inevitably raising children with a man who didn't see life the same way I did. I'd have done it. I'd have made it work, but it wouldn't have been the life I secretly longed for in my heart. Looking back, it was such a bad fit. But I'd loved him.

Yet here I was, at my mother's behest, consuming a ransomed lunch with this man in a three-piece suit and feeling more relaxed than I had in a long time.

After lunch, he walked me home. I stood in front of the quaint second-floor Newbury Street apartment that doubled as my home office and said goodbye to someone who, at face value, was not at all my type, but whose soul resonated with mine.

I reached to shake his hand.

"Hugs are better," he said and pulled me into his embrace as if it were nothing.

That hug changed my world.

In that moment, when the earth stopped spinning, I knew I would marry this man. Peter was *the one*. Truly, deeply, and inexplicably.

How could I be so sure of something like that based on...a hug?!

Was it intuition? Was it a premonition of the future?

Could I permanently end an engagement built on seven years with a man I'd loved dearly despite our faltering—not failing—relationship? My fiancé had been the safe choice. But not the best choice.

That earth-shattering hug had flashed the possibility of a better life. A life where I was known and understood, empowered and given space to be who I was meant to be. I could raise children with someone who saw the world the way I saw it, a true partner who could and would urge and support me to live the way I, Patti Giuliano, was meant to live.

I could break things off with Jerry and live my truest life with Peter. But not before the universe had a little "fun" with me.

After three weeks and several unsuccessful attempts at arranging another date, I stood in my home/office after a serendipitous lunch with a financial planner, Steve, who'd mentioned that he'd grown up with Peter.

"You know Peter Kevorkian?" I'd asked after my jaw dropped to the floor. Then I asked Steve if Peter had any girlfriends.

"Hundreds," he'd answered with a smirk.

Returning to my office after lunch, I resolved to forget Peter. And maybe bite the bullet and crawl back to marry Jerry.

Minutes later, the phone rang.

Guess who?

Three weeks later, on our second date, an actual "official" date, we wandered through Harvard Square soaking in the moonlight and chatting. I didn't attempt to hold his hand, though I deeply wanted to. After years of having such affection reproved, I had muted my instinctual desire for intimacy. This wistful realization hit me in the space between our fingers.

But Peter wasn't Jerry. He was different.

As we approached a puddle, he offered, "I can carry you across. So you don't have to get your shoes wet."

I'd followed my intuition from a relationship where publicly holding hands was totally unacceptable into one where I was literally swept off my feet.

Holy shit! Who knew?

If you were judging our chance of success as a couple by the ways we dressed, we didn't look like we belonged together at all. But five months later, on September 18, 1983, we married.

Forty-plus years later, I still have no regrets. Had I not listened to my intuition, I would not be the same person today. I would not have been the same parent, and my kids, whoever they might have been, would have had an entirely different start to life.

My intuition had been right, and I had listened. Thank God.

***

Right about now, you might be thinking, "I thought this was a parenting book, not a love story."

It still is a parenting book. I promise.

Our choice of life partner, if we are blessed to have one, sets the stage for what is arguably one of the hardest, most important, and hopefully most rewarding journeys of our lives: parenthood.

It was, and continues to be, for me.

This moment, this love story made the difference between a life of empowerment and a life of struggle, a life of giving to a profession I loved from a place of wholeness and a life of divided loyalties and attention. My choice made possible a life in which I could parent my children the way I knew I needed and wanted to. Parenting is so much easier with a person who gets you, who calls your best self forward, who encourages you, whose values are aligned with yours, and whose soul resonates with yours.

You could say that Peter was my match made in Heaven. But he was only the first of three. Peter and I had two children, and I learned that every child, no matter how frustrating, challenging, adorable, loveable, easy-going, or different, is a perfect match for their parent. I believe that every parent and child set is, in some way, also a match made in Heaven.

My love story with Peter is one of intuition, the first of the simple ingredients in our parenting recipe.

I do have the answers inside me. I, like all of us, possess an intuitive sense that deserves trust. We need only remember to listen and feel—and act upon the knowing given to us.

I have had other moments of deep knowing, for sure. But never before or since have I taken that great a risk in following my intuition with all my heart and soul, trusting that this was my path, my future, and that it would all work out.

I'm so glad I did.

Some say intuition is a gut feeling, a hunch, or a divine inspiration that comes through us. Others say it is learned from previous experiences. I believe it's probably a little of both, but with a greater emphasis on the former.

Haven't you heard of a parent's funny feeling that something has happened to their child preceding a phone call that they have been in a car accident or worse? Have you ever made a decision without checking all the facts and details just knowing it was the right decision?

Besides meeting my husband and knowing I would marry him, my intuition informed me what to say to defuse my daughter when she was trying to jump out our second-floor window (more on that later). One day, while working in the office, my husband had a sense that something happened to one of our kids ten minutes before receiving a phone call that our daughter had taken a softball to her face and had a concussion.

Among the many gifts of being married to Peter is that he calls to something deep inside of me, something that draws me to reach for more. In that hug, he pulled me into a deeper relationship with my intuition. And he still does.

Life-altering moments are not always as dramatic as that lightning-bolt hug. Some are so subtle that you can't pinpoint them. They are realizations so gradual or incremental that you only recognize them after the fact. They have immense power, too, because they allow us to trust ourselves more and more with each experience.

When we become aware of these brilliant moments of inner knowing, we must mark, celebrate, and remember them. Preserving their impact and importance strengthens our intuition so we can better identify its signal, amplify its quiet voice so it breaks through the noise of everyday life with the power of a state-of-the-art sound system.

If you need a recipe where every ingredient is spelled out with exact measurements, you may be having a hard time with my suggestion to trust intuition in life. Especially as a parent.

It's scary! I get it.

But I invite you, I challenge you: try.

Got a big decision to make? Slow down. Listen to your body and your gut.

I changed my grandmother's recipe—risking a fate worse than death in my Jersey Italian family. Of course, I waited until Sabaluche passed before I'd even consider it, and she is probably rolling in her grave. But it worked out—and better than I expected. All who have sat at my table would agree.

I made the recipe my own, starting with intuition, and used it to nourish my family so they could all grow to be their best selves.

Coffee Break

A Morsel of Peter

"Today you are You, that is truer than true.
There is no one alive who is Youer than You."

- Dr. Seuss, *Happy Birthday to You!*

I have written this book in the first person, from my perspective as a *mom*, particularly as a cis-gendered (as my editor explained is an important distinction), heterosexual mom raised in a particular time period and parenting in a particular time period. As you read, you will see there are a lot of *I*, *me*, and *my* usage. In wanting to acknowledge and be authentic to my experiences, I need to take a moment to emphasize *I did not parent alone*. Not for one minute! In every *I*, *me*, or *my*, know that Peter, my husband, was an integral part of the decisions I made, the experience I had, the parent I was, and the parent I became.

We did this parenting gig *together*! (Thank the Lord!)

Peter is my rock, my beloved, and my parenting partner. We shared every moment of every day BC (before children) working beside each other in our home chiropractic office practice. People always want to know how we could survive together twenty-four-seven. Did we ever get sick of each

other? Did we ever contemplate murder?

We have had our moments. For sure. But early in our relationship, we figured out that we have our lanes where we work best, and we work hard to stay in those lanes and not encroach on the other.

For example, I do the cooking, and Peter makes dinner reservations or orders takeout. And we are very good at what we do. I'm a *justa-watcha me* kind of cook, like my grandmother taught me. With a look in the refrigerator, I can create a gourmet meal, while Peter needs to have a recipe and follow it precisely. This follows our parenting styles. I am not a big planner. I tend to listen to my gut and feel my way through many situations like my mother before me and my daughter after me. And Peter, who was an engineer before he was a chiropractor, will (like his dad and my dad and our son) plan everything to the last detail.

I'll have a great idea like, "Hey Peter, why don't we have a party?"

"Great!" he'll reply. "When, where, what time, how many people, and what do you want to serve?"

"Holy shit, Peter, that's a lot of questions," used to be my response in the early years.

If it was left to me—and many times it was; I'm such a party animal!—I would call and invite people a few days before the party and ask them to invite other people we know. I'd go shopping a day or so before, decide what we would eat while I was shopping, come home, realize I'd *thought* I had vanilla but was mistaken, and then either have to be creative with the cookie recipe or send Peter to the store at the last minute.

Peter, on the other hand, will make lists. He will send invitations weeks ahead of time, plan the menu and shop days before, set the table, and make sure we have matching table settings down to just the right wine glasses and napkins folded Martha Stewart-style. And if things did not match, he would go shopping to complete the set. If we'd be grilling, the grill would be checked for propane and the utensils cleaned and ready for use.

We have done it both ways; neither is right or wrong. We both follow our intuition and our patterns of how we see things; we just do it differently. I don't always look at the bigger picture/outcome. I go with what I am feeling at the moment and the feeling I want people to have. Peter will look at what outcome and experience he wants for the group. Regardless of how the planning and prep happened, we have had some *amazing* parties! And in all honesty, when I adopted some of his planning and he relaxed some of his anal tendencies (LOL), we both found that we had a more relaxed and better experience in the prep phase and more time to socialize.

And so it was with parenting.

Not that many people would call school planning a party, but when we were evaluating the best schools for our children, we leaned into our strengths in a similar way. Peter would list all the schools, who we knew at them, the pros and cons attending each school, and he would collect and present all the data we needed to evaluate if the environment was a good fit for our family. I would be the one to call the faculty, take lead in sit-down interviews and visits, and ask friends, family, and others to share their experiences to get a *feel* if it was a good match.

We complement each other's personality traits and we are in absolute alignment with our values and philosophy. Our parenting styles were similarly a little different, yet we always acted out of a united front. Peter was more likely to stay inside and play board games with the kids while I usually played outside games or took them swimming. Even our circadian rhythms are different, but we work to complement each other.

I remember one morning at 6:30 AM—the middle of the night for me—when a little hand tugged on my covers.

"Mommy, Mommy, I'm hungry!"

I half-opened one eye to see my adorable three-year-old son beside the bed. I managed enough coherence to say, "Christopher, go downstairs and tell your daddy. He will get you something to eat. Mommy needs to sleep."

Were it Peter (and he weren't already awake), he would have jumped out of bed without hesitation and made breakfast. I, on the other hand, was perfectly willing to stay up as late as (and sometimes later than) 2:00 AM to write out birthday cards for the office or watch a movie or Johnny Carson. Or do both simultaneously. Years later, I'd be helping with late-night homework challenges or taking our daughter's calls from across the country.

Mind you, when I did wake up (sometime after 10:00 AM), I felt horrible! What kind of mother was I to not get out of bed to feed my child?

While Peter thought it was hysterical at the time, he didn't throw me under the bus. He never made Christopher think I was a bad mom for not getting up.

As I was told later that day, Christopher walked into the office in his PJs, went up to Peter while he was adjusting a patient, and said, "Daddy, I'm hungry. Mommy told me that you would get me breakfast."

After he and the patient had a good laugh, he said, "Christopher, your mommy needs her sleep. I am happy to get you breakfast as soon as I am done with this patient."

He has used that story many times (granted, with kind humor) to illustrate and emphasize my boundaries as Not A Morning Person to our kids and patients. He explains that it's best not to ask me anything before 10:00 AM because it's not my "most resourceful time."

And, in turn, after 8:00 PM, I step up because that's not Peter's "most resourceful time." It all works out!

Parenting requires an acknowledgement of different styles and the ability to adapt and jump in when one of you has a challenge that the other has the skill set to respond to in the spur of the moment. We tolerate a lot and are forgiving of our differences. Otherwise, I don't think we would have made it this far.

The most important thing is our philosophy and values were completely in alignment and that got us through some of the major challenges that we faced as a couple and as parents.

While Christopher was away at Delphi Academy in Oregon, we received a call from the ethics officer. Christopher had gotten around the school's firewall and downloaded a movie that was not within the "acceptable" boundaries of the school's ethics code.

I was immediately embarrassed and freaked out. Our son was headed down a path detrimental to his well-being! He was going to end up a criminal or a psychopath or *something worse* in my hyperbolic Italian imagination.

Peter took the whole thing in stride.

Which, of course, only infuriated me more. How could he be so *calm* in the face of *our baby boy* doing something that would ruin his future?!

"Patti, I promise you, this isn't as bad as you're seeing it. Please, hear me out. I have a plan..."

One of the things I love about Peter—once I'm over my initial rage at his natural cool and logical demeanor—is his soothing and charismatic nature. He's very good at inspiring people to listen. So after my Jersey Girl tantrum, I was able to hear his point.

Our son had an uncanny knowledge of computers that would be an asset to him in the future. He just needed to focus his skills in a positive direction. (And thank God he did!)

My husband is my best fan and my biggest cheerleader. His spirit is in every story of every page of this book—and just like in parenting, he was there for me whenever I wanted his input, required another trustworthy viewpoint, and needed a loving embrace during a mental or emotional breakdown. He could have written this book, but he loves it when I do the cooking, so he let me be the one to plan this party to share this recipe with you.

Chapter Four

Philosophy: An Evolving Foundation

*"You have brains in your head.
You have feet in your shoes.
You can steer yourself any direction you choose."*

- Dr. Seuss, *Oh The Places You'll Go!*

"Are you crazy?"

I heard that question a lot in 1987 when I told people I would be giving birth at home. I had a few choices in that moment.

I could smile and simply say, "Knowing me for all these years, do you honestly think I would do anything on earth that would put me or my baby in harm's way?"

Or I could let the Jersey Italian come out and deliver them a few choice words.

Want to guess which path I took?

I get it. We all have our belief systems and perspectives that we acquired throughout our life. Sometimes we go with what we learned and don't ever question if it is our own belief.

Me? I questioned everything!

My parents weren't too keen on me asking "why" and "why not" all the time, so I got into trouble a lot!

Yet they were nonconformists, themselves. They did not trust the medical establishment due to errors made by various professionals that had detrimental effects on family members and friends. They were followers of Adelle Davis and Edgar Cayce. Davis was an American writer, nutritionist, and advocate for improved health through better eating. Cayce was a clairvoyant and proponent of eating whole, preservative-free foods. We took vitamins, ate healthy, and went to the chiropractor regularly (not just when we were sick or had symptoms). We practiced "preventive" medicine or "wellness care" depending on what part of the medical community you spoke to.

When we did have symptoms, my mom assessed the situation, and most of the time, she'd just smack us up the side of the head "Italian style" and tell us, "Go outside and play" or "Go to school. You'll feel better."

Most of the time, we were faking it because we had a test or incomplete homework. Except when we didn't. Then we stayed home, were given castor oil (an Edgar Cayce recommendation), and stayed in bed, wrapped in blankets until our fever broke.

We learned our bodies were smart and knew how to heal themselves without any outside intervention. We were not fussed over for every little ache and pain. My siblings and I learned to trust our bodies. Likewise, we were taught to think critically, to be creative and self-sufficient.

So when it came to being pregnant, birthing our babies, and teaching our children our values and beliefs, I relied on my childhood lessons. I wanted to be in control and not have anyone tell me how I should do it. If I wanted to birth my babies in a tub of water and my husband agreed (which he did), then I would find a way to do it and be sure it was safe. After all, I had heard the story of my own birth so many times that I was prepped for the experience.

While rushing to the hospital, my mom had to cross her legs to prevent me from popping out in the car. I was out within forty-five minutes of her water breaking. The only drug she had was a short sniff of ether applied to her wrist from a cotton ball.

I was prepared. For whatever birth brought and whatever judgment would be flung at me for my birthing choices.

I had data that the questioners didn't have, which allowed me to justify my decision. And I *normally* look for alternatives to the status quo. I analyze situations and information, and then see if they fit into my personal philosophy and belief system.

So what do I mean by philosophy and beliefs? This idea I keep referencing?

"Philosophy" is a whole study on how we understand life with many layers and definitions. For the purpose of this book, and my usage, I'm talking about one's personal philosophy of life: What is our overall vision for our lives? What is our attitude toward life? What is our individual purpose in life?

"Beliefs" are just as complex a term with many contradicting meanings. But I told you I like simple, so for me, simply, my personal belief system is based on these two questions: Why do I hold this philosophy? What is the best action to live within my philosophy?

We all possess a philosophy and belief system that dictates how we view the world and the actions that we take. Yes, you have a philosophy, even if you just wondered, *"Do I?"*

My philosophy, backed by experience and research, is that we, humans, inherently know what is best for our bodies. As I mentioned in my "On Pregnancy" interlude, I'm a *vitalist*. I believe our bodies have an innate wisdom and brilliance about how to best *live*: how to survive, adapt, and thrive in the surrounding world. If our bodies, minds, and spirits are aligned, we are best at our own healing. I'd spent my life fostering my intuition, listening to my body, and educating myself as a chiropractor to help bodies function at their maximum potential.

The best place for me to bring life into this world was where *I* was most comfortable, with the experts I trusted most, where I would best hear my body, and where this new little person could begin life with a holistic and healthy relationship with their body.

So if your life's philosophy calls you to do something differently than societal standards and expectations, as mine called me to explore at-home birthing, if it calls you to take a leap of faith, before you make a decision—because people will say, "you are crazy"—I encourage you to:

1. gather good data to support your decision,

2. think about whether it fits into your way of viewing the world (your beliefs and philosophy), and

3. think about the impact your decision will have, not just on you, but on all the people who may be involved.

Then take action with confidence.

My philosophy, as any philosophy should be, has been—and still is—an evolution. It involves my parents' beliefs, the environment I grew up in, and what I choose to believe from my life experience. I don't accept all that my parents, relatives, and teachers taught me, yet I don't totally reject everything either. I take what fits closest to who I believe myself to be and the direction I want to go in my life, and then I work at living true to my beliefs.

Back to my "crazy" decision to birth at home.

Our first plan was to birth our child and place her in a bath immediately after birth (the Leboyer Method[2]). Imagine being a newborn that has never experienced life outside the womb coming into this world, getting their head squished, getting exposed to lights for the first time, *and* it's 20 degrees colder?

What a shock! We didn't want that for our baby.

As we read more on the subject, we came across Sondra Ray's book, *Ideal Birth,* which introduced us to underwater birthing and its benefits for gently transitioning a baby from the womb into the world.

I immediately thought, *That's crazy!*

How would the baby breathe? How long did they stay underwater? Was it safe? Would our midwife be open to the idea and qualified to support us? Would I be brave enough to do it?

So, we did our research.

When I Googled "water births" while writing this, I found about twenty-two million results in 0.45 seconds. Back in 1987, we didn't have access to that data, and water births were not so common. We had books and videos. The more I read and the more I watched newborns swimming after being birthed, the more my left brain was convinced. I thought, *I could do this.*

What would we need to make this happen?

First, a birthing tub. We bought the only tub that we could afford that would fit in our tiny house: a horse's trough. Very inexpensive at Agway Farm Supply.

Where would we put this horse-trough-turned-birthing-tub? The only practical place was in our bedroom, which was already a tiny room, but it was the closest to the bathroom (less than ten feet away, which is a loooong way when you are in labor!). We also needed a hose to reach from the tub faucet to fill the trough.

Next came finding a skilled and qualified midwife who would support us with the tools necessary for a successful birth.

What if something went wrong?

People asked, and to be honest, I asked myself that same question. How did I handle it? We were in a home birth birthing class at the time, and the leader of the class, Cathy Romeo, compelled us to think about the worst-case scenario. She prepared us emotionally and physically for the possibility. Thanks to her wisdom and the skillset she provided, we were prepared for the possibility of needing a hospital transfer.

So we took action. We visited our local fire department and informed the EMTs about our birthing plans, asking them to be on call should we need them. They were very curious and agreed to be on call.

We chose the rest of our birthing support team and educated them on the process and their roles. And Peter and I continued to educate ourselves about all the physical, emotional, and spiritual aspects of birthing. The book, *Spiritual Midwifery*[3], by Ina May Gaskin, was our bible throughout the entire home birth process. The stories of women in a small community in Appalachia having successful home births gave us the motivation and the support to know that we were on the right path with our home birth decision. Most importantly, I needed to know down to my very core that the safest place for me to birth my baby was at home and have all bases covered.

If my home birth had been a disaster, it might have crippled my ability to follow intuition or even my own judgement in the future.

So, at about 11:00 PM on that fateful May 4, it felt like my body just exploded. Water came gushing out all over the bed. And probably all over Peter.

"Here we go!" I said, jumping up and running to the bathroom.

My whole life had been gearing up to this moment. I was so excited, utterly unafraid of the pain that would follow.

After monthly, hour-long sessions with my midwife, going over every detail, learning, planning, and chipping away until my fears weren't scary anymore, there I was, sitting on the toilet, feeling the unrelenting, intense urge to push.

"Holy shit! I can't do this for hours! I can see why people take drugs!" I yelled at Peter.

But my faith was unwavering. I held onto my philosophy and beliefs. I would get through to the other side if I just trusted my body.

I was on the toilet maybe fifteen minutes when Peter, who was on the phone with the midwife, said, "Patti, Jami can hear you and says it sounds like you should get into the tub."

Holy shit, already? I'd heard about my fast birth my whole life, but all I could think of in that moment was how comfy the toilet felt. I didn't want to move!

"Jami says, 'Do you want to have the baby in the tub or in the toilet?'"

To respect my more sensitive readers, I won't repeat my exact words to Peter. Reluctantly, I lifted myself off the toilet with Peter's help, left the bathroom, returned to our bedroom (the longest ten steps in my life), and got into the tub.

And just in time!

I had *no earthly idea* what I was in for.

This perfect baby, who I had envisioned a million times, exited my body into the water within one and a half hours after I'd jumped out of bed.

And then she took an *eternity* to breathe. A few cracks began in my unshakeable faith.

The world stood still until we heard that first precious cry. All that apprehension melted away. She would be fine. She would be perfect—"perfect" as I naively imagined.

Nope.

That unshakeable faith? It was about to get tested harder.

In my part of the world, every newborn gets an Apgar score to measure their health immediately after birth. Out of the ten points indicating how well she transitioned from the womb, she only scored two.

My long-awaited, precious baby arrived with a stark lesson: our journey together would not be a journey where I was one hundred percent in control. There were *two* people in our mother-daughter relationship. In seconds, she drove this point home.

As I look back at the three decades we have walked together as mother and daughter, I realize my daughter has been my greatest teacher. She started from her first breath. She wasn't the "perfect" newborn I'd so naively imagined. She was—and is—*Katie*-perfect.

We were the right parents for her. She was the perfect daughter for us. We had no idea how to live that truth.

Yet.

***

After that fateful spring night, I had to adjust to a different truth, an evolved one.

My choice about birthing Katie at home, informed by my philosophy and beliefs, was the right choice. Having an assumption about some "perfect" outcome, however, needed to evolve. I had a vision of my life and the life I'd share with my children.

My children needed to develop their own philosophy, as I had, and that meant they got to create *their* own vision for *their* own life. Starting from how they decided to exit my body.

But also, I needed to re-evaluate my idea of "perfect." My *truly* perfect life might not be what I *assumed* "perfection" would be. Starting with what it meant to be a "perfect" parent.

I needed to realize that I was *exactly* the right mom for my kids, even though failures were inevitable. Parenthood wasn't going to be this blissful, easy ride that I'd imagined.

We would navigate this together: Peter, Katie—eventually Christopher—and me.

Chapter Five

Unconditional Love: A Deeper Connection

"I had to learn to forgive myself, not to judge, but to learn from the past. They showed me how vital it is to accept, be truthful, and love myself. So I could do the same with others."

- Marlo Morgan

"What are you doing, Katie?" I shrieked across my teenaged daughter's second floor bedroom.

"I'm going to jump!" she screamed from beside the open window.

Imagine this scenario. I never did! Not in my wildest nightmares.

Not ten minutes prior, I'd been standing in my kitchen having a screaming match with a very teenage, very opinionated daughter. (Not sure where she got *that* trait.) When the argument reached a peak—to this day I can't remember what it was about—she stormed upstairs.

Come to think of it, not all that differently than when I stormed out of the laundry room somewhat recently. Hmmmmm?

But Katie didn't return to the kitchen. Before a few minutes passed, I heard loud thumping and banging upstairs. I went to investigate.

Now we're back to me shrieking and her about to jump.

Holy Shit!

I stood frozen in my teenaged daughter's doorway, heart pounding. I don't know how I found the air, but I shrieked, "What are you doing, Katie?!"

My thirteen year-old daughter stood on a chair propped up next to her bedroom's casement window, ripping the screen.

Paralyzed, I watched wood and metal fly everywhere.

She had one leg out the open window when I came to my senses. Might I remind you, we were on the second floor. I ran at her.

She screamed back, "I'm going to jump!"

What in this particular argument had caused this crazy, over-the-top reaction? I had not a clue, nor was I thinking about that at the moment. All I knew was my baby girl was trying to jump out the freaking second-story window!

I had to stop her!

I yanked her away from the open window. Pieces of wood clunked to the floor as she screamed for me to let her go. I pinned her to the bed with my hands and knees.

She struggled underneath me.

Inches from her face, I yelled, "What is wrong with you? Are you crazy? Why are you doing this?"

Either she was unresponsive from the might of my hold or I was so enraged, screaming so loud that I couldn't hear if she did say anything.

We were pinging off each other's energy like atoms in a nuclear reactor.

I snapped out of it after a decade crammed into maybe two minutes. She was not moving, and in my altered state I wondered, *Had I killed her?!*

Stunned and in shock at my actions, I climbed off and headed for the door in a daze, probably to get Peter's help.

As if in slow motion, Katie jumped off the bed, turned toward me, and screamed the words every parent shudders to hear: "I *hate* you!"

I paused in disbelief and horror. My impulse was to fire back some nasty "I don't care, go ahead and hate me..." kind of a statement.

But her words woke something deep within me.

I was a child again, getting a beating for some disagreeable comment I'd made. *It's not fair!* I'd thought. I'd just needed to know they loved me even though I'd made a mistake.

I *didn't* want Katie to "go ahead and hate me."

It wasn't my job to manage my daughter's emotions. It was my job to manage mine, to share my calm instead of joining her chaos, to be a rock of unconditional love *even* when that was hard. Even when it meant taking the proverbial "high road" and not retaliating.

Oh, if I could say I did that every time we had our challenges, I'd be lying. I was not always a kind, loving, Zen mother with all our altercations. And that's okay. We are human. But I only vividly recall the times I caught myself before I did something I'd regret. Selective memory is such a blessing!

This was one of those times.

My heart spoke to me. *Stop. Soften. Act out of Love.*

I changed my posture (hard to do in fight or flight, ready to flatten the threat—my precious daughter in this case). Dropping my voice to reflect the peaceful state I had accessed, I spoke the most unnatural but most important words I could into that situation.

"I'm so sorry, Katie. You can hate me if you want. But I love you so much. I will always love you, no matter what."

I can't remember if she cried, but I did. And she didn't jump out the window.

In that moment, I was vividly aware I loved her from deep within my soul. It was palpable.

I know she felt it; she knew it was sincere and real. And I was so grateful to access that little-girl part of me that wished her parents had responded to her anger and chaos from that same loving place I'd shared with Katie.

To this day, Katie has never again said she hated me.

And she certainly has had many chances.

Our kids, these beautiful creatures we've created, can hurt us so much, so easily. Their spirits are connected to us like no other. And when their words reveal our inner wounds, it rarely comes at a convenient time or in a gentle way. An unwelcome bolt out of the blue smacks you with a "WTF was that about?!" that calls into question your very sanity and ability to be a parent.

That moment with Katie was nothing short of divine intervention. I realized *I could lose her!* Sad as this may sound—and I am not proud of this—that may have been the first time I'd connected to my *unconditional* love for her.

I had told her I loved her many times, but always with conditions:

I'll love you if you let me get a complete night's sleep.

I'll love you if you don't cry.

I'll love you if you play nice with your friends.

I'll love you if you don't talk back to me, if you let me comb your hair, if you do well in school…

And on and on.

Feel free to add your personal favorites to this list. Parents, can you relate to me?

Holy shit! My life was changed. Love. *Unconditional* love.

***

How many conditions do we put on the people around us? It's not just me, right?

Without realizing it, we apply conditions to love all over the place, but especially to those closest to us. Family members. Spouses. Children. Why? Because we believe they will forgive us? Maybe. But will they forget? Who knows? One would pray for that.

And ourselves. How many conditions do we put on loving *ourselves*? If I can keep my temper… If I make sure to exercise enough and always eat all the right foods… If I just balance my life, my career, my spiritual journey—oh and the schedules for a household of busy people, as well as an office staff…

If I can do all that perfectly, I love myself.

"Whaddaya, stupida?"

If it isn't obvious by now, the all-important ingredient to my parenting recipe, the key to becoming—always *becoming* because the journey doesn't end—the best mom I can be for my kids, for *me*, is love. *Unconditional* love.

No, it doesn't come easy. At least not for me. Unconditional love requires work, requires us to go deeper into ourselves, our souls, so we can *Stop. Soften. Act out of Love.*

In an ideal world, we would always love ourselves and our kids unconditionally. The latter is arguably easier. We don't have to like everything our kids do and say; we just have to remind ourselves that we love them *no matter what.*

Loving ourselves, though—*that* can be hard.

Consider this, though: How would you react if someone spoke to your children or your partner the way your worst inner voice speaks to you? Would you put up with that?

I can tell you what this Jersey girl would do! Or not. Plausible deniability is important.

One thing I've learned—okay, I'm *still* learning—is as we love ourselves, we are able to love others beyond our wildest dreams. I don't know if I heard someone else say that first, but the whole sentiment just flows out of me naturally.

When it comes to parenting, it's imperative that we be kind and *love* ourselves. Unconditionally. Or at least aim for that. We are human, after all, and so are our kids. We're going to screw up, all of us. We're going to get pissed off, we're going to say hurtful things, and we're going to seriously regret some of our decisions.

Stop. Soften...

Find that hurt, angry child raging against all that is unfair—the one hiding in our hearts or glaring across a bedroom disaster—and remember all they want is to know they're loved.

Unconditionally.

When all else fails and everything's gone to shit, remember the greatest force on the planet, the most important ingredient in *every* recipe, is *love*.

Coffee Break

A Moment of Weightlessness; *Katie's* Window Story

*"Vulnerability is about showing up and being seen.
It's tough to do that when we're terrified about
what people might see or think."*

- Brené Brown

I didn't see anything wrong with what I'd said.

Mom and I were either agreeing with one another using different words or having a discussion of two or more different topics, thinking it was only one topic. Either way, I remember Mom ending it and I went up to my room for some space.

I was greeted by four large windows, two facing east and two south. The open windows invited the crisp air in, creating a serene atmosphere.

An idea sparked in my mind—a window bench, or even better, a deck outside my window. I imagined myself sitting on the banister, legs dangling off the edge, embracing the feeling of weightlessness.

Drawn to the window facing the door, I removed the screen that served as a barrier against bugs and perched it

precariously on a chair. The screen wobbled as I climbed the chair to the window sill, making a loud noise.

The sensation of being high above the ground washed over me, bringing a sense of focus. I slipped into a meditative state.

A thought crossed my mind: *I could jump.*

The adrenaline surged; my heartbeat quickened. Would I die if I jumped? Would it hurt? I didn't want to, but the thought of being weightless felt liberating.

My family would be creeped out, I concluded. *I should come off the sill.*

A gust of wind blew past my ears and knocked the screen over with a *bang!*

Strong footsteps approached. My mother entered the room.

Afraid she'd misunderstand my motives, I blurted out the lie, "I'm going to jump!" I hoped that would keep her in the doorway.

Other words were spoken as she approached, but I dissociated, overwhelmed with all the emotions I felt: my own and what I was reading from her. I moved into a dream state.

As we exchanged words, I felt drugged and invalidated. It had been *my* idea to come off the ledge, not Mom's!

Through that mix of emotions that kept me from being able to dismount, my mom's hands grabbed me. Feeling like we were dancing, I allowed her to move my body to the bed. It felt like flying, like being weightless. I went along with it, hopping as she lifted me from the floor and onto the soft mattress. Like jumping on a trampoline, I was propelled up, higher than I would on my own.

Her concern pierced into my consciousness. The dance ended, and I was pinned. The lack of movement was uncomfortable. A laugh briefly escaped me as I felt a warm rush. I expressed my desire to be let go in clear English and quick tugs, but she refused. So, I focused on the parts of my body that felt weightless.

Closing my eyes, I felt my body get heavy and my eyelids start to flutter. In my mind's eye, I saw the face of a tribal

monkey mask superimposed where my mother would be. I struggled to hear what the mask was saying. I dropped into a deeper meditative state; mattress and covers enveloped me. I softened my muscles to the bed's embrace as the words became clearer.

So did a feeling of unconditional love.

The mask became faint for a moment.

I was struggling to separate what thoughts and feelings were mine from what I was picking up from my mom. There was a brief stillness in my perception, but it wasn't sharp or clear. There were my thoughts, my emotions, my mom's thoughts, her emotions, the situation, the sensations from the dissociative state of mind—that weightlessness I'd felt, then lost, and then felt again. I was experiencing and observing all of this at the same time and some feelings more than others.

A thought, faint, distant, and shy, came through the mask I was envisioning. *I killed her?*

Uncertainty loosened my mother's grip.

As I'm writing this, I'm aware I've read my mother's version and it could be influencing my own memory, but I recall wanting to ask if she was coming from a place of love.

And then she let go. I could still feel her presence in my dissociated sense of consciousness, like a fog that had filled my thoughts.

Freedom brought with it frustration, confusion, and anger at our actions. Were these my feelings? Or hers?

What were my feelings? Shreds of that sense of unconditional love began peeling off like a husk. A sadness grew in me as I felt a loss of connection and an untethered *weight* of concern.

I wanted to express everything I was feeling and how she was wrong to act as she did—taking away my agency, my choice to remove myself from the windowsill. As the fog dissipated in my thoughts, the pull of separation was like stretching Silly Putty with a snap. Ending the connection, words sporadically exploded out of me.

I recall saying or meaning to say "I...don't...hate you," consciously whispering the "don't." I think, somewhere

between my conscious and subconscious, I wanted her to feel the ambiguity I felt. She had misunderstood and misconstrued something I'd said and something I was doing, so maybe I would regain some control by purposefully creating something she would misunderstand. "I... hate you!"

After a moment to gather herself, she came back and apologized, assuring me of her love.

Per her version, she said, "I'm so sorry, Katie. You can hate me if you want. But I love you so much. I will always love you, no matter what."

If you'd asked me before I read her version, I wouldn't have remembered those exact words.

What I do remember is I still felt weird. The normal and expected thing would be for me to say that I felt loved and appreciated, but to be honest, I remember feeling like her words—probably the assurance of love "no matter what"—still suggested I'd done something wrong. Why would I need to be told I was loved "no matter what" unless I'd done something that might make her not love me?

I did appreciate the apology, and in retrospect, looking at the big picture, I can also say that her unconditional love gave me the freedom to experience the full range of my emotions, however contrary or contradictory they were. I can look at things now—this experience and others—with the ability to accept that, in any situation, people can get stuck in feeling hurt and misunderstood because I was able to have that experience, knowing I would always be loved.

Coffee Break

Different Teachers

"Gratitude is one of the sweet shortcuts to finding peace of mind and happiness inside. No matter what is going on outside of us, there's always something we could be grateful for."

- Barry Neil Kaufman

Up to now, you've mostly heard me speak about my daughter, Katie. Even before my firstborn came into the world, she was teaching me with more "Holy Shit! moments" than I ever expected.

And she continues to do so to this day—possibly even as you read this.

In this next chapter, I get to introduce you to my son, Christopher, and the *very different* lessons his spirit had— and still has—to teach me. My son is a more quiet and gentle teacher than my daughter. He was softly teaching me while in utero, like Katie, but his birth made abundantly clear the kind of teacher he would be—and *holy shit*, I desperately needed those lessons right then. (Even though I didn't realize it right away.)

What I learn from Christopher is no less important than what I learn from Katie, but my lessons from Katie tend to

be...let's say *louder*, shall we? And *perhaps* more challenging. One of my biggest worries as I was composing this book was that I have more stories about Katie.

When you look back at all your learning, isn't it so much easier to recount the hardest lessons? The ones you *really* had to work for? The lessons you may not have *wanted* to learn at the time?

If I've said it a hundred times before—and I have—I'll say it hundreds more times: Katie and Christopher are my and Peter's greatest creations! Both of them, together and separately, equally in their own unique ways.

Two distinct spirits, two completely different types of teachers: How can one "simple" parenting recipe feed such drastic needs?

Let me tell you about how Christopher was born...

Chapter Six

What I Wasn't Expecting

*"Life isn't about how to survive the storm…
It's about how to dance in the rain."*

- Vivian Greene

Has anyone told you that you don't need birth control while you're nursing? Don't believe them!

The only way you don't get pregnant is if you don't have sex. Obviously, Peter and I didn't follow those rules, because fourteen months after Katie was born, I started vomiting every day and that little blue dot appeared again. Nine months later, after only forty-three minutes of labor, our son, Christopher, came into the world the same way Katie had: a horse trough in our bedroom. We were in the same house, which was beginning to feel a lot smaller with a toddler running around.

And going to a hospital was still off the plate after Katie's "close to perfect" home birth.

In the twenty-three months between them, the horse trough had transitioned a few more babies from the womb to the outside world—and gotten a few upgrades! Pool noodles with slits down the middle now lined the edges, and there was a blow-up pillow to rest your head while laboring! *That* was an especially wonderful addition, even though I didn't really need it much for yet another short labor and delivery.

Even more helpful, one of the other families had added a pump for emptying the tub when the birth was over. I wish we'd thought of that! The tub was too heavy to lift while full, and it's not like we could open the drain hole onto our bedroom floor, so after Katie's birth, we'd emptied it one bucket at a time out the door, over the deck railing, and onto the grass below. The grass was a little gross, but after a few rainfalls, there was no trace of the blood-tinted water left behind.

Anyway, we were much more prepared this second (and hopefully last) birth, and thank God we were!

My water broke at 8:02 AM. (I am *not* a morning person!) I jumped out of bed and headed to the bathroom, where I stood in the shower, hanging onto the wall for dear life. Fluids drained from my body with intense contractions.

Similar to Katie's labor, the contractions were nonstop!

Peter started filling the trough and called the midwife and support team.

Peter's sister, Christine ("Auntie Chris" to Katie), was given the job of Katie's caretaker. We wanted Katie to witness the birth of her sibling with some boundaries, and we knew Auntie Chris would keep Katie happy during and after the birth with as little interference as possible.

Once again, everything happened so quickly!

I was unaware when Auntie Chris or anyone else, except the midwife, arrived. I was in an altered state. I was escorted by someone —probably Peter—from the bathroom through those very looong ten steps, over the three-foot edge, and into the tub at 8:30 AM.

And then all I remember was pushing nonstop while the midwife encouraged me to slow down. "Don't push so hard. You don't want to cause tearing."

Tearing the perineum, that bit of skin between the vaginal opening and the anus, was one of my biggest fears of childbirth. Besides being incredibly painful and requiring stitches and more healing time, it could lead to infection and serious complications later. In preparation, just as I'd done during Katie's pregnancy, I'd regularly used olive oil massages to soften and stretch the vaginal wall and perineal area. It had worked for Katie, and I was hoping it would work again.

Because those contractions and the pushing was so intense!

All of a sudden, I felt the comfort of the warm water on my lower body and my pain lessened.

It worked! The prep, the coaching… All of it together worked!

Christopher popped into the tub at 8:45 AM. Forty-three minutes after my water broke! All my parts were intact. Incredible!

To this day, my husband jokes, "Patti, if we had a third baby, we would probably find them at the bottom of the bed when we woke up."

As Christopher was exiting my body, I remember saying, "There really was a baby in there." Pretty bizarre, right?

We've even got that bit of brilliance on tape!

While Katie arrived hours ahead of schedule and we didn't have anyone available who knew how to use the video camera, we ("we" meaning Peter, the engineer and planner) were prepared for Christopher's birth. My son arrived on schedule, in the morning, so we had the photographer, the videographer—who did a great job of keeping the video PG while capturing the essence of birth (and my brilliant commentary)—extra helpers, and plenty of supplies on hand.

It sounds silly, but I was so preoccupied with caring for Katie twenty-four-seven that it had barely registered I was pregnant. When Christopher finally arrived, I was shocked out of my delusional state.

As much as I was focused on birthing Christopher, I was still aware that Auntie Chris was being challenged in her task of allowing Katie to be part of the process while also keeping her from jumping into the tub.

Peter and I strongly believed if Katie could see her brother enter this world, she would bond with him. We'd heard stories of babies brought home from the hospital to a sibling who'd had no idea where this new person came from, and therefore, had a hard time bonding.

Katie's repeated cries of "My baby! My baby!" with increasing agitation and volume, along with her need to join the process *in the tub,* was not exactly the bonding experience we'd envisioned.

Eventually, Auntie Chris was able to divert Katie's attention enough so everyone could leave the room. Peter and I could have a moment alone with Christopher.

I sat back in the tub, and Christopher was put on my stomach.

Peter, who'd shared the tub with me for both births—coaching me, supporting me, applying pressure to relieve some of the pain in my tailbone, and catching both babies as they left my womb—held us both as I nursed our son for the first time. This was Christopher's first chance to get our full and undivided attention in nine months. This was my chance to finally acknowledge his presence. This new, precious being would need our attention—my attention—and love.

If you have ever worried that you might not have enough love to spread to more than one child, I can tell you this moment convinced me of the infinity of love. When I looked at Christopher for the first time, I cried for joy, overwhelmed with deep emotion and love for this spirit. I no longer worried I wouldn't have enough love left for another child!

A deeper part of me still wondered: Would he be all-consuming and need my undivided attention like his sister?

Christopher's first lessons to me were just beginning.

Unlike Katie at birth, Christopher's coloring was good, and he started breathing immediately. His Apgar score was 10. He barely cried, and when I lifted him to my chest, he started nursing without a problem. He was already a different baby from his sister.

I was on an adrenaline high, happy to lie back (with that lovely pillow) in the warm water, nursing this new and different baby.

My state of bliss was sadly interrupted.

Atma Kaur, my midwife, entered the room and said, "Patti, you need to birth the placenta."

I stared at her, trying to process her request. Finally, in the kindest voice I could muster, I said, "Atma Kaur, it will come out when it's ready to come out. I trust my body!" I was done pushing. End of story.

After forty-five minutes of coaxing (two more minutes than it took to give birth), I finally agreed to push a few more times to get the placenta out.

Unfortunately, by waiting so long, it was stuck, so Atma had to reach up inside of me with her tiny little hand (thank God) and pull it out of me. Not a great experience. I mean, I had never had anything other than her hand go *up* there like that (okay, no Peter penis jokes here), but I *had* had two very big heads exit, so I was *sorta* familiar with the sensation? I am not recommending it, so if you are asked to push out the placenta, respond quicker than I did or suffer the embarrassment and discomfort.

After *that* interesting experience, I was ready to get out of the tub. My body was all shriveled up from being in the water so long, and I was freezing, even though the room was eighty degrees. As I headed toward my bed with Christopher still attached to me, I felt the warmth of towels wrapped around my and Christopher's bodies. (Thank you, *thank you*, my wonderful midwives!)

I handed Christopher to Peter, who was reclining on the bed, while I put on my bathrobe.

I was ready to make breakfast for everyone!

But Christopher wasn't having it. Peter's nipples weren't producing milk, and he wanted us to know he was still hungry! I joined Peter on the bed, and Christopher reattached himself to my breast. Beside us, Peter teared up with emotion, smiling with so much love and joy that I started crying too.

Out of nowhere, Katie burst into the room, appeared on my side of the bed, and wanted to nurse. Christopher was on my breast near her, so she tried to push him off to make room for herself.

I could have pushed her away from me, but I didn't. I could've asked Auntie Chris to come and take her out of the room, but I didn't.

Instead, I moved Christopher to my other breast and let her join us. I was in a high adrenaline state and ready for anything! Katie had twenty-three months to prepare me for this, and I remember thinking how this would make a good story someday.

If it seems strange to you that Katie was still nursing close to two years old, it was common practice among my circles to nurse their kids until they left for college. Well maybe not that long, but at least until three, four, and some up to five years of age. So, I allowed Katie to nurse alongside of my newborn boy because it was the one thing that calmed her down during the first twenty-three months of her life. And I didn't need any tantrums at this moment.

When I settled into a comfortable position with the two of them nursing, I looked at Peter, he looked at me, and we both started laughing hysterically.

"I feel like a cow!" I managed between laughs.

And then I realized this may be a foreshadowing of Christopher's life: having to share his mommy with his sister. A sister that was going to have a hard time sharing her mommy with her new baby brother.

Holy Shit!

How could I be the unconditional loving parent refereeing two children who would each need my undivided attention?

And also give enough love and attention to my husband?

How would I care for all of them and still have time for myself? Fulfill my calling as a chiropractor?

This scenario was not in any of the parenting books I had read nor did any of my friends or relatives give me a clue that all of this would be so hard to navigate.

Hours after Christopher's birth, Katie was still vying for her nursing position on one breast while Christopher was on the other. My new baby was being initiated into the world of Patti, Peter, and Katie, with Katie demanding the undivided attention of the rest of us. Christopher was learning how to share this loving space with a very determined spirit.

Meanwhile, I was getting anxious about how I would survive with a second child that would not sleep. And then, Christopher slept through the night from day one.

I was prepared to nurse him twenty-four-seven, as I had done for Katie. And then, Christopher nursed when he was hungry and stopped when he was full on a schedule we could plan around.

I was preparing for him to be inconsolable. And then, Christopher cried and fussed only for specific needs.

It was like he intuitively knew that his sister needed more attention, and he was willing to give her the space to get what she needed. How could he know that at such a young age? While there is data that indicates babies can hear and sense things from inside the womb as well as respond to and be affected by the chemicals that are flowing through their bloodstream while in utero, my intuitive sense tells me he was prepared for this adventure long before he was born.

The stress chemicals I must have emitted, the sounds that he'd heard, and the prayers that I'd whispered... "Please God, give me strength to be the best mother I can for both my children. Give me the patience to endure whatever challenges may arise. Please give me a child that sleeps!"

Holy Shit!

What was happening? Could it really be the answer to my prayers?

Unbeknownst to Christopher, with just him sleeping through the night consistently, I realized I *could* survive this new challenge! It *would* all work out.

I just had to realize and accept that Christopher would bring me on an entirely different journey I *hadn't* planned for. I was willing to accept almost anything, as long as I could get some sleep!

***

My babies may have come from the same parents, the same genetic pool, and yet they both arrived with their own spirits and personalities. They were born into the same environment, but each brought their own unique needs, challenges, and gifts.

Peter and I were still the perfect parents for them, and they were the perfect children for us, but we needed to learn what, exactly, that meant for our lives. What that meant for us, each of us, as people.

When your resources are depleted and those you love need that love expressed in utterly different ways, how can you be unconditional in that love?

I would *love* to tell you that, once you learn this parenting recipe I'm sharing, everything will fall right into place and things will get easy, but I'm not going to lie to you. We're people; *people* are not infallible, and that's all right. In fact, many people are especially gifted at screwing up the most "foolproof" recipes.

Fortunately, some of our greatest lessons come from the most spectacular screw-ups, so long as that's how we look at our screw-ups —as lessons.

The good part of having a dependable recipe is that, even if we mess up, we have the ability to try again. We have the groundwork to figure out what ingredient we missed or mis-measured or tried to substitute without success. If our situation has changed, maybe we're at a higher elevation or lower humidity or something we don't even perceive. We might have to adjust the recipe to fit that situation.

Case in point: Christopher and I started baking together when he was under ten years old. We *loved* chocolate chip cookies, and we were excited when someone gave us the secret recipe to the famous Neiman Marcus chocolate chip cookies.

Our first time using that recipe must have been so stressful to Christopher because we didn't have all the exact ingredients, and he is a lot like his father when it comes to cooking/baking—he likes to follow the recipe exactly. I, being a creative baker, insisted with much passion that we would be fine if we altered the recipe a little. I wanted a more "natural" cookie, anyway. Organic whole wheat flour, organic chocolate chips, maple syrup instead of white bleached sugar, and organic butter. And we were going to add walnuts (not in the recipe).

"Christopher, our cookies are going to be better than Neiman Marcus, you'll see," I promised.

They weren't!

They were flat and crispy, not moist and thick like we like them. Our creations, sadly, were not nearly as good as old-fashioned, run-of-the-mill chocolate chip cookies. Later, we realized we had also added too much baking powder—because not only did I alter the recipe, we doubled it and screwed up amounts. WTF!!! We still ate them.

The next time we followed the recipe exactly and made the most awesome cookies.

"See, Mommy, it works better if we follow the recipe."

"Yes, Christopher, you are right! But we had so much fun, didn't we?"

He agreed to that and didn't make me feel *wrong* for the choices I'd made.

When you've got two (or more) very different children, the recipe still works: Intuition, Philosophy, and Unconditional Love mixed together, kneaded, and prepared with the intent of nourishing everyone involved. But you need to be open to learning new ratios, mixing strategies, and exploring new applications of the ingredients.

Christopher was the "perfect" baby according to everyone (including me). He didn't cry all the time, he slept through the night, and he was always smiling. But this "perfect" baby offered new and different challenges. Within a few weeks of his birth, nursing had become painful for me. My nipples were starting to crack and bleed, and Christopher had white cottage-cheesy stuff in his mouth and on his tongue.

Holy Shit!

I called the midwife, checked in with La Leche League, and found out I had mastitis and he had thrush! Mastitis is an inflammation of the mammary ducts, and thrush is a fungus that can develop during nursing. I learned both are very common among nursing mothers but never talked about for some reason. Until it happens to you, and suddenly you have a new awareness of it. And then it appears *everyone* has gone through it. Kind of like life!

(For newer parents, I strongly suggest you find a lactation consultant, so you have a resource for such surprises. I've included information on La Leche League International in my resource library at the end of this book, but check online, at your doctors' offices, at libraries, at community women's centers, and more for what will work for you.)

The typical treatment would require me to stop nursing so I could heal.

Bottle-feed my babies?! That was not going to happen! I had done the research. Breast feeding has so many positive benefits to a baby's health and longevity, such as passing on antibodies, bonding, better posture for the babies, and lower instances of asthma and obesity. I was willing to do anything to continue and be the sole source of my babies' sustenance until they were ready to show me signs that they wanted to eat solid foods!

Looking back, I wonder how rigid some people must have perceived my thinking. Maybe you do as you're reading this. Hell, I'm thinking that right now. But here's the thing, I learned!

I'm not saying I changed my philosophy and beliefs—far from that! My philosophy is to learn everything I can and to trust the wisdom and genius of my body. My body was telling me things needed to change! I (eventually) accepted I needed to honor that, and with the help of Peter, my community, and friends, I discovered other natural options that honored my beliefs about what my body needed and what my children's bodies needed to not only be healthy, but thrive.

What did I do?

First, I had to look at the whole situation as a learning experience. What was my body telling me it needed? What tools did I have to give my body what it was asking for? And, like how pregnancy symptoms prepared me for caring for my children outside of my womb, what future challenges of motherhood was my body preparing me for?

Mastitis is inflammation. I'm a doctor; I have many ways to address that! And as a chiropractor, specifically, I wouldn't mask the pain for short-term relief. It would be better to endure some pain and give the body the chance to heal. In doing so, I am acknowledging and monitoring the symptoms. In my awareness, I can better hear what my body needs to heal, and as it heals, my body will learn this new skill—in this case, how to heal mastitis.

And heal I did.

Aren't bodies awesome? I think so!

Before and after I nursed, I bathed my breasts in Epsom salts. Let me tell you, that was a bitch! I applied vitamin E to the broken skin and cursed *a lot!* I wanted to slap Christopher, but that would have been cruel. He didn't intentionally cause this! I accepted this was preparing me for more challenges in life and a motherhood that would require me to pay attention to my body, to not forget to care for it, so I could be strong enough to care for my loved ones.

After all, as a new mom, I'd made a commitment that I would strive to be the best I could, and it would require some sacrifice on my part.

Was it easy? Hell no. But I believe it was the best choice for me and my body.

Fortunately, Christopher was very patient with me. I cried a lot when I nursed him. When the pain was too much, I stopped and gave my breasts a chance to heal before I nursed again. He nursed less during that first week, and I healed very quickly. (He made up for it in the following weeks. Even a three-month-old body can adapt!)

I was learning Christopher wasn't the male Katie. He was and is uniquely *Christopher*.

Later, however, I had more health challenges (keep reading for those stories!) and I eventually had to let someone else feed Christopher. The choice was heartbreaking in the moment—and I fought it—but I accepted the change because I was still adhering to my philosophy: Christopher was getting the benefits of breastfeeding, and I was listening to what my body needed.

During this time period, I also needed to stop nursing Katie while my nipples healed. We started giving her watered-down juice in a bottle and she had been eating solid foods for the past year, so I knew she was getting the nutrition she needed.

Was it the "perfect" nursing experience of motherhood I'd envisioned? Nope.

Another important lesson from these challenges with Christopher's nursing? My job wasn't to define and impose "perfection" on my children, my household, or myself. My job was to follow my grandmother's recipe: listen to my intuition, honor my beliefs, and make my decisions out of unconditional love. In fact, the love was *truly* unconditional because I wasn't forcing us to fit into my expectations.

(Confession: We're not even halfway through this book, so I assure you, this lesson about trying to force things into my expectations is one my kids and the universe regularly smack me with!)

I believe that everything and everyone that comes into your life has a purpose and a meaning. I find blessings even in the most unfortunate of circumstances. That's who I am.

Christopher's entrance into our family taught me I was not the cause of Katie's challenges upon her birth or how she experienced the world. I had done nothing wrong, I hadn't eaten or not eaten the right food, I hadn't made any grave mistake in birthing that had harmed her or damaged her being.

I was not a bad mother!

Life brings us many challenges and lessons. Growing up, whenever I had challenges, I constantly heard from my parents that, "God, or whoever you believe to be the creator of this universe, doesn't give you anything you can't handle." Personally, I am sick of God thinking I can handle so much crazy shit.

But on the other side of all the crazy shit, there's always a lesson to be learned or a blessing that prepares us for the next challenge. Maybe I needed all those lessons and blessings? Maybe the world needed me to have learned those lessons so I could share those blessings with others? I don't know.

What I do know is if you are a parent, the challenges don't stop. They just change. With each situation and with each child. So be open to those moments of *holy shit*, their lessons, and the blessings they bring.

Be prepared for a change or ten in your dinner plans and recipe execution.

Isabella Laterza Carola (AKA Grandma Lizzy or Sabaluche) probably swearing at the person taking the picture while forcing a smile because they caught her in her house dress and apron in the street outside of her house. Almost as bad as sitting on the "stoop." Her love was infused in her food: She was the best cook, and she made sure you let her know when you sat at her table.

Chapter Seven

Communal Eating: It Takes a Village—Or a Team

*"When you walk to the edge of all the light you have and take
that first step into the darkness of the unknown, you must believe
that one of two things will happen: There will be something solid
for you to stand upon, or, you will be taught to fly."*

\- Patrick Overton

My grandmother made her cooking look so easy. Her recipes were so simple. Her life was so simple.

Or so I thought!

As I got older, it became apparent that she actually spent the *entire* day cooking these "simple" recipes. From the comfort of her metal kitchen chair where she reigned, she would regularly pull herself up to address a stove with every burner filled with her masterpieces. Wooden spoon in hand, she would check each pot and pan, stir, taste, and add more spices or other ingredients as needed.

She didn't appear to have (or need) help. After all, most of the time we went over to eat, everything seemed ready to be served. Yet, as soon as we stepped in the door, she started the list of orders:

To me, "Poddi, metta la tavola!" (Patti, set the table!)

To my mom, "Cealia, go downa stairs anda getta the vino!"

And before that, unbeknownst to us, layers of help and

contribution unfolded from the family and her community.

For pigeon cacciatore (we—at least I—didn't know it was *pigeon* cacciatore at the time, either), Joe Ferrone had found the bird in the street that morning and brought it over as a gift (because if she hadn't already done some favor for his family, he knew she would). So, free protein she didn't have to buy to feed our large family!

She may have boiled, skinned, and defeathered the bird herself, but she'd called my father (who worked a block away) and had asked him to ask my mother to pick up vegetables for her at the store. Both my uncles had stopped over for three o'clock coffee and biscotti—and had changed lightbulbs, moved furniture, or handled any other heavy tasks my grandmother would've needed. Then my Aunt Gerry would've stopped by after work to check and see what else my grandmother might've needed. And would have done it, of course.

Invisibly sewn into the family and community dynamic, my grandmother had a lot of help. And she had no problem asking for it.

Because I didn't necessarily see all the help my grandmother had —and I perhaps didn't necessarily see my mother sending my siblings and me to stay with various family members as her asking for help (nor any help she received from other family while we were away)—I was convinced I shouldn't have to ask for help on my parenting journey.

All I needed was the right recipe, like Sabaluche had! And then everything should be perfect.

I can hear you laughing. I know.

But why *couldn't* I just follow a simple parenting recipe and have everything be perfect?

Because what goes into preparing a good meal is so much more than just the recipe!

Even as I write this, knowing that I probably had more responsibilities in a day than Grandma did, I feel like I was not as well-equipped as she was. She lived in a community where her job as a family matriarch wasn't all that different from that of her mother before her. Not only did she get the "training" on how to ask and what to expect for help, but my family and the neighborhood shared those same expectations of each other. Families stayed close; neighbors knew to share resources—be they ingredients or hands working.

When I was beginning my parenting journey, I was in

Massachusetts, my mom and dad were in New Jersey, and my sisters were in Virginia and New York. My friends weren't on my block or even in the same town, and they all had their own lives and their own kids—and I never heard them complain!

Why was I finding everything so hard?!

The only answer that makes sense to me now is that I was trying to be the *perfect* mother, the *perfect* wife, and the *perfect* chiropractor all at once and all the time.

And in not being *perfect*, I was failing at all of them.

I can hear my grandmother's words now: "Whats-a matter for you? Are you-a stupida?"

After Christopher was born, I became a zombie. Not because of *him*, but everything that goes along with having two children under two years old.

And wanting to be the *perfect* mother of *perfect* children.

My time and energy needed to be increased for two children instead of one. Nursing two instead of one. Diapering two instead of one. Tummy time and every other something-time activity to stimulate their brain and body development for two instead of one.

I am exhausted writing about it.

I longed (with a lot of guilt) to get back to being a chiropractor, a job that I had mastered. A job with many rewards in each interaction. A job that I did without question or hesitation, without worrying I was making the right decisions. I was confident and capable in my profession.

With less than two years under my belt as a mother, I was struggling and questioning my abilities.

I'd expected (optimistically? foolishly?) that if I followed the "simple" recipe I'd thought I'd learned from my grandmother, I would know how to respond to my kids and all their needs perfectly. I'd use the knowledge I learned from experience (i.e. living with my mom, aunts, and grandmother; reading books, listening to mentors—and watching *Donna Reed* and *The Partridge Family*), and then after filtering it all through my philosophical beliefs, I'd check in with my intuition, and *then* if all that failed, so long as I loved them unconditionally, everything would be perfect. (Phew, that was a mouthful!)

Yeah, right! In a *perfect* world, maybe.

But how could I complain? Grandma and my mother each managed with four kids. My Aunt Josephine had five kids. My college friend came from a family of *nine* kids, and her mother was still sane.

What was wrong with me? I only had two!

The reality? I am a different person than the mothers of my mother's and grandmother's generations. I grew up in the sixties when women were exercising their independence and showing their strength—that they could run a household while working full time. I wasn't going to be "just" a housewife like my grandmother, mother, and all my aunts. My generation of women were looking to be recognized for our equality with the men in our society.

We were going to show them! We would become "super" moms: work full time outside as well as inside our homes.

Holy Shit! What were we thinking?

Back to Christopher's entrance into our family...

After he was born, I was waking up several times in the night to nurse Katie, who slept on the mattress next to our bed (while Christopher slept next to me), and then waking up early in the morning to Christopher needing to nurse. I tried to meet my own simple needs of going to the bathroom and making breakfast for myself (which didn't always happen).

And a shower? I was lucky to take one every other day while Peter watched the kids.

And diapers—

Did I tell you I only used cloth diapers? I was willing to do the extra work to rinse and wash the diapers myself (or use a diaper service) in order to have cotton be used on my "perfectly natural" children's bottoms. I didn't want to use synthetic materials against their bodies. After all, I only wore cotton and other natural clothing for my own health; I would do the same for my kids. There was enough data to convince me that I was making the right decision. It was less expensive to use cloth diapers rather than buying boxes of disposables. Ecologically, I was not contributing more dirty diapers to landfills. I made a lot more work for myself, but I was convinced it was worth it.

Returning to my daily routine as a mother of two under-two-year-old children...

At some point I had to make lunch for Peter and myself, do the food shopping, take the kids outside for a walk, wash clothes, keep the house clean and decluttered, etc., etc., etc.

And damnit, I *missed* being a chiropractor!

I remember my dad calling me one day when my mom had to fly to Ohio to help my sister with her second baby. He started the conversation with, "I don't know what you women complain about. I don't know what you do all day."

"What do you mean, Dad?" I asked with some measure of disdain.

"I just had to wash my own clothes for the first time in my life, and all I had to do was put the clothes in the washer, along with the soap, and push the button. Then I come back thirty minutes later, and they're done. Then I throw them in the dryer. It doesn't take me any time at all to do that!"

"Reeeally?!" My heart was pounding and my face was red. "Did you have to stop folding the laundry while your kids were crying for your attention? And while you were putting away that laundry, did you have to change a few dirty diapers? Oh, and while you were cleaning the house, did you remember to feed the kids, make lunch, make sure there were clean dishes for dinner, and then, a few hours later, make dinner for the family?"

"Whoa, stop there!" he said. "I thought I was going to get sympathy from you, and I realize I called the wrong person."

I may have been frothing at the mouth at this point. "*Really*? And who do you think you can call for sympathy because every other mother—" (Very few dads in the 80s were stay-at-home dads.) "—you call will want to jump through the phone and strangle you!"

He quickly said his goodbyes and hung up.

I sat down and cried.

My dad actually did me a favor. He gave me a *Holy Shit!* moment. He opened my eyes to what I expected of myself. Why *did* I think I could do it all by myself?

Let me pause here and reiterate I have the most supportive husband on the planet. I wasn't doing it all alone. We had our chiropractic office downstairs, and if I needed him, Peter would be up in a flash.

But I thought doing all of these things was *my* job, and *I* needed to figure out how to do it all or I would not live up to my vision of the perfect mother and wife!

I felt guilty that I was not able to manage this new way of life: parenting two children.

One *Holy shit!* moment wasn't enough though. The universe had to basically give me a big whack up the side of my head to open my eyes.

Interesting how the universe does that, though!

One morning, I woke up with an excruciating headache, vomiting uncontrollably. Very unusual for me, and utterly unexpected.

I didn't have time for this!

Christopher had just turned four months old and Katie had just turned two. I'd already gotten through the whole mastitis and thrush ordeal. And while Katie had almost entirely stopped nursing and was eating solid foods, when she unraveled, latching back on to nurse was the only thing that calmed her, so I was back to tandem nursing.

I was even talking to Peter about coming back to the office a couple hours a day!

While I was in the bathroom vomiting, I could hear Christopher in the bedroom crying uncontrollably. I was unable to respond.

Peter heard the commotion and ran upstairs from the office. Realizing Christopher needed to nurse and I was not in a position to accommodate him at that moment, Peter jumped into action. He took both kids into the office and had patients help keep them occupied. Although Christopher had never had a bottle, they gave him a bottle with watered-down juice until I was available.

When my vomiting stopped, I attempted to nurse Christopher. Within seconds, he projectile vomited my breast milk! Something was very wrong: a testament to the wisdom and genius of his body. I was toxic, and it was making my breast milk toxic. His little body knew it and rejected it!

As the day continued, so did the headaches. I felt numbness and tingling in the right side of my face. Then my whole body started to feel numb, and I had no energy.

I'm having a stroke! I thought. *I'm going to die, and my kids will lose their mother!*

In the bed after another vomiting session, realizing there was nothing left in my stomach to heave up, I started crying inconsolably. My head was pounding and I couldn't stand up on my own.

In between sobs, I asked, "What is wrong with me, Peter?"

Peter was by the side of the bed holding my hand, and trying to comfort me. "It's going to be okay. Your body is going through some toxic reaction—"

"You don't understand!" I shouted back despite my head feeling ready to explode. "I have never ever felt like this before. It feels like I am going to have a stroke, and then who will take care of you and the kids?"

My wise husband knew better than to respond while I was in such a hysterical state. Still holding my hand, he just listened.

I continued my rant, but at one point, I remember interjecting, "If I die, please don't marry Jane Smith!" (Name changed to protect the innocent.)

Peter still tells me he had the hardest time keeping a straight face while he said, "Patti, you're not going to die, and I can't even imagine marrying Jane. She's so not my type!"

I was in a health crisis. It felt like a near-death situation; I *never* get sick! I could only assume this was a worst-case scenario: I had a dreaded disease or I was having a stroke. The numbness in my face and side was getting worse as the day went on. My head still threatened detonation, any attempt at movement shot piercing pain down my arms and legs, and even if I *wanted* to move, I had no energy to do so.

I didn't have time for this!

My baby needed breast milk, and mine was not healthy for him. I couldn't nurse him if I tried. I had nothing left to give.

As I mentioned in the prior chapter, when I went through the experience with mastitis, breastfeeding was a priority for me and many women around me based on the long-term and short-term benefits to our babies' health and well-being. Would it have been easier for me to abandon my philosophy and start bottle-feeding formula? I don't know. I know many women can't and don't breastfeed for a number of valid reasons, and they are no less good mothers for following their philosophy, intuition, and unconditional love in making that decision. That just wasn't the right choice for me.

What do you do in those situations? When the world is out to get you, you have no control over anything, and you think you're dying, what *can* you do?

Rally the troops!

I needed to, for sure, but even in my dire circumstances, I bristled against that reality.

I had many friends. The ones with kids seemed to be managing parenthood with ease. I hated them for that—no, not really. But I was wondering if there was something wrong with me, and now my body was failing me.

I was in a predicament. My kids, especially Christopher as a four-month-old, needed to nurse. What to do? I had to be creative. Could my friends, who seemed to be managing parenthood better than me, be able to help? What would they think of me asking for help? Would that be weird? Probably! Would they judge me? Maybe! Would I be burdening them? I didn't know!

I was in a desperate state without any other options.

I am a resourceful person, and even in this bad state that I was in, I knew there was a solution. I had heard of mothers purchasing breast milk from a milk bank. But I wouldn't know who it came from and that deterred me from going that route.

Could I get breast milk directly from a source I trusted?

Two of my close friends whose daughters are the same age as Katie were still nursing. What's the worse they could say? No?

I called M* first. "Hey M, I need your help. I am flat on my back and there is something very wrong with me. Christopher is hungry and is crying hysterically. I tried nursing him, but he projectile vomited my milk. Can you help?"

I didn't even finish speaking when M said, "I'll come over right now. My milk supply is over the top and my daughter is not nursing as much."

After a few days, and not knowing how long my body would be out of commission, it was clear that M could not do it alone.

I called my other friend, K*. I didn't know her as well as I knew M, so I was a little more verbose. "Hey, K, I am not sure if you would consider... And you can say no, and it is okay. Is there any chance you would be willing to help me with Christopher? I've been too sick to nurse. Do you have any breast milk in your freezer that you would be willing to share? M is nursing him for me and she can't do it alone."

"Absolutely!" she answered without hesitation.

I couldn't believe my ears! "Did I hear you right?"

"Better yet," she offered. "I will nurse him for you if you want."

"You will?" I'm sure I was about to cry.

"Absolutely! Put your energy into getting better, and M and I will make a schedule to take care of Christopher for you."

They were both happy to help! *Holy Shit!* All I'd needed to do was ask. Even though they were my friends, and I knew they would help if asked, I never wanted them to think I was less than perfect. I mean, how could I let myself get so sick? It was hard, but I was so sick I had nowhere else to go.

I realized—well, I kinda already knew—they were as crazy as me! Would most women outside our circles do the same? I didn't know. It was a *big* ask, and I was so grateful.

I spent two weeks bedridden, feeling like I was going to die, but my babies were nursed by two angels!

But my two angel friends weren't enough for all the things that needed to get done while I was out of commission, so my husband rallied the family. Peter called my mom and dad!

I was too weak and miserable to argue. I'm not sure what he told them, but they drove up from New Jersey and were here the next afternoon.

My parents and everyone else who came to help were sort of invisible to me. I slept most of the day, and when I woke up, I vomited. For two weeks. Nonstop. I caught glimpses of my mom playing with Katie and my friends nursing Christopher. My dad was fixing things around the house and driving my mom to the grocery store when needed. They were a tremendous help, and Peter could continue seeing patients, knowing the kids and I were in good capable hands.

After his long day in the office, Peter would come upstairs and, without complaint, play with and care for the kids. He would give them baths and put them to bed. Then he would sit up with my parents for an hour or so before he came to bed. My mom kept my family well fed!

All this happening while I was lying in bed, just about helpless. Feeling guilty.

How was it so easy for him? What was wrong with me? Why couldn't I be the perfect mom I'd planned? Why, oh why, oh why?

As I healed from what I call my "near death" experience, I explored what might have been the cause. I did not have a "medical" diagnosis, just specific symptoms I could analyze: tingling in one side of my face that traveled down my right arm; a headache like I'd never had before, like someone had me in a vice grip; severe pain in my neck with any movement; blurry vision; nausea; and brain fog. Also, my digestive system was not functioning properly and my breast milk was toxic. By all counts, it looked like and acted like a stroke—but it wasn't!

One possibility presented to me by a spiritual counselor and RN, Collette H.*, was that my Kundalini energy got stuck around the third chakra and needed to be cleared. She gave me the book, *A Kundalini Experience, Psychosis or Transcendence* by Lee Sanella, MD. In his years of practice, Sanella had worked with people presenting symptoms that mimicked those of heart disease and stroke without having the actual disease; they were suffering from blocked energy!

As I explored my life, I came up with my own possible explanation. My body had shut down because part of me wanted to be *everything* for my kids and part of me resented them for keeping me from my life's work and passion—taking care of patients as a chiropractor. I couldn't resolve those conflicting parts. My guilt and the universe forced me to STOP. Full stop. Of *everything.*

I needed to figure out what I *really* wanted and what I needed for my survival (and that of my children and husband). I was given a chance to process this conundrum. Not willingly. But did I mention I could be stubborn? So can the universe.

As a result of my brilliant discovery of needing balance, a better plan, and that I *couldn't* do *everything* myself, Peter and I adapted our schedule so he could be with the kids a few hours a day while I returned to the office to regain my sanity and my independence. And, thank God, I was back on my feet within three weeks after the pseudo-stroke experience.

Our plan eventually evolved into us finding someone we trusted to watch our kids for a few hours in the evening so we could both be in the office together. That made us happy. My emotional state shifted drastically. I didn't realize how depressed and resentful I had become until I was able to see my life from a different vantage point. I needed some distance from my babies to see that I was making myself sick trying to be the perfect Super Mom. I needed to integrate being a mom and a chiropractor for my health and that of my family.

***

After going through mastitis and then the pseudo-stroke, I was wondering what next?

Christopher was the "perfect" baby when he was born, he slept through the night, and yet I was still being challenged to my core.

The whole experience, the good and the bad together, was the blessing I needed at the moment. I had to realize that nothing in this new parenting experience would ever be perfect!

Peter lovingly teased me, "You thought you had it easy with him. Christopher is not even half a year old, and he is preparing you for when he gets older and doesn't need his mommy any more."

"That was so mean, Peter! He is always going to love his mommy and never leave her, so stop saying that!" I would joke back—*sorta* joke back.

Letting go of old beliefs and patterns—such as toxic independence and not asking for help—sometimes comes at a high price. Even if these things don't serve our personal philosophy and beliefs, they can be so ingrained in our upbringing and old teachings that we don't realize we can release them. That not only are they not essential to our being, but they conflict with the person we truly want and need to be.

When life brings us challenges, we need to be able to look at them squarely and change course or direction. For example, if my grandmother didn't have enough onions to complete her onion pie recipe, she would add other vegetables or cheese to make up for it, and create a new and wonderful dish. Or she might send someone down the street to the corner store, ask another family member (remember we all lived within a few blocks of each other), or send one of us kids to ask a neighbor to borrow the ingredient. Sabaluche wasn't hesitant to ask for help. As a matter of fact, she demanded it! Parenting requires adaptability and creativity, and part of that is to rely on your "village" when the *Holy shit!* moments come fast and furious.

***

It takes a village to raise kids!

A village, a community, a support system—

Find your kindred spirits, your "village," and rely on them—and be ready for them to rely on you. It works both ways: That pigeon cacciatore? You can be sure some got delivered to the Ferrone family

—along with other meals my grandmother would cook.

Now we're getting into the *secrets* of how you make a "simple" recipe work for you and your family. Every chef has a few up their sleeve—and some (like me) might even share those secrets with you. I gave you the "simple" recipe in the beginning of this book, and then I explained the ingredients—told you it was adjustable to what you and your family need. Now we're getting into the nitty-gritty! The secrets of *how* this recipe works.

And having help—sous chefs and kitchen staff if you will—is the first one.

Because it's the secret you've seen without *seeing*.

As I was growing up, did I hear my grandmother giving orders around dinner? Did I hear family members mentioning they stopped by and did a task? Did I hear about a neighbor giving my grandmother some ingredient? Did I help pack and deliver meals or ingredients to other family members or neighbors?

Sure!

Yet I was *convinced* all these mothers had done everything themselves—so therefore I should! Not only that, but I'd do it *better*—while also having a career!

If you find yourself in a situation like I was, and you, like me, feel like you should be able to do this alone, please reach out to friends, family, or maybe an organization for help. (If you don't have available friends or family or know any organizations, I've listed several I trust in the back of this book.) If nothing else, reach out—

But, *no*! I will not come over to your house and cook and clean for you. Been there, done that! Or as my own mother says, "Did. Done. Don't wanna." Healthy boundaries, right?

(You can check my website for more articles and references, though!)

My hat goes off to single parents. I thank God that I have an amazing husband who has kept me sane during the hardest parenting times. I don't think I could have done it alone! Actually, I *know* I couldn't have done it without him.

I had (and still have) an amazing group of friends. When Peter and I moved to Westwood in 1984, we looked for a spiritual church where we could eventually raise kids, one with inclusive values and principles aligned with ours. We were blessed to find a nondenominational church in town with a couple young families who shared our beliefs about health and raising kids. Many members of our church became patients after they got to know us and understood how chiropractic benefited health care.

We were still closest to our chiropractic friends. Two of my friends from chiropractic school and I had started a mastermind group in 1982 that met weekly to support each other as we started our practices. All three of us had spouses who were also chiropractors, but Peter was the only one who attended our meetings; the other two spouses (women) stayed home with newborn babies. Those moms began feeling left out because they weren't able to practice with newborns, so we restructured our meeting plans to accommodate spouses and parents, as well as open things up to other chiropractors.

One Sunday a month, we gathered at someone's house or office and held a pot luck (healthy options only). By the late 80s, the group had grown to between fifteen and twenty chiropractic families, and by the early 90s, the baby population of our group had grown. After six girls, Christopher had the notoriety to be the first boy to be born after the group formed!

We shared philosophies about birthing, breast feeding, health care, and parenting, which was so important to all of us. Many of us birthed our babies at home, some even sharing the same tub that Katie and Christopher were born in. We used the same midwives and gynecologists who were amenable to our home births. We didn't all make the same decisions about how we parented our kids, but we shared the same "recipe" (even before I coined this idea for the book) of trusting our intuition, holding to our philosophy and beliefs, and consciously striving to make sure our decisions were based in unconditional love. Each of us adapted these practices to our own children's needs. It was and continues to be a blessing to have all those friends in our life.

That being said, not everyone in your support group needs to come running when you call for help. Find your "besties"—one or two people who you know will drop everything and come running if there is an emergency or can help you troubleshoot. (And who you'd do the same for!)

For many years, our community, our "village" of families

gathered socially once a month. Our children grew up together, like cousins, and we parents relied on each other for advice, support, and friendship. We trusted each other implicitly. When there was an issue Peter and I were not able to handle or if we needed more data, we called our friends, our chiro family. Several of these friends were there to help welcome Katie and Christopher within twenty-four hours of their births! They filled me in on things like how to best nurse, how to make the cloth diaper fit a newborn, and how to take a nap when the baby naps. These are things you don't know until you know.

Despite having this amazing circle of friends and "besties," as well as my family, I'd still hesitate to ask for help when I needed it. Over and over! Shit! I would be calling them every day, twice a day if I'd known then what I know now. Not only for my health and sanity, but because—I eventually realized—they were probably going through many of the same challenges as I was, despite my perception that they weren't having any problems. They may have had solutions to things I didn't think of!

But I didn't want to appear to be helpless or needy or incompetent. I figured I had my husband to bounce challenges off of, so why did I need the other women?

Confession: It took me *over twenty years* to realize there were insights I get from my female friends that I can't get from my husband or their husbands. Duh!

Interestingly enough, I, myself, was always volunteering my help no matter how busy I was: run an errand, watch a friend's baby, help in a friend's office, or stay late for a patient.

In those early parenting days, the few times I did ask for help, I had much less stress and found myself a more loving and conscious parent. I was able to allow the ingredients of my parenting recipe to blend together more smoothly. Another *duh!* And every time I asked, I was always met with an affirmative response. I remember one of my friends saying, "Patti, you know when you allow someone to help you, you are giving them the joy that you feel when you help others. Don't hold back."

Holy shit!

I was depriving others of happiness if I didn't allow them to help! In helping me, they could feel the blessings I felt when I helped others. Who knew?

Hopefully, this will help you to allow others to reciprocate at a younger age than it took me. I finally got real good at asking for help in the past few years. Some of us are slower learners. (Yes, I am implicating myself very lovingly.) It takes as long as it takes.

*****

As we entered the school years, in the late 90s, our group slowly drifted apart. We were all enmeshed with our practices and the demands of busy families.

Organically, Peter and I became friends with other chiropractors from New York, Pennsylvania, Georgia, and New Jersey who we met two to three times a year at seminars where we could bring our kids. As our friendships grew, we took a leap and became vacation buddies, spending summer vacations together. Our parenting styles blended together because they also used the same "recipe" we did.

It began to dawn on me that it was a universal recipe that worked for all types of families and all types of kids.

There were anywhere from five to seven kids among us on vacation, and they were all unique. Each needed different parenting skills. We learned from each other and were grateful for the wealth of knowledge we could share as a group. Our vacations with our kids (or parenting therapy sessions, as I would call them now) have changed into adult vacations. The kids, some of whom are married, will join us if it works in their schedules, but it is usually us parents who have maintained our vacation outings.

And those monthly Sunday potlucks from the earlier 90s? We may have drifted apart while our families and practices had needed more of our attention, but now we're back to getting together once or twice a month. Since we're not chasing kids around, we often meet for dinner at a nice restaurant, or better yet, we plan dinner and game nights.

And what do we talk about? We ask each other advice about life and impending retirement, finances and trips we are planning. And sometimes we talk about our grown kids.

Who am I kidding? We *always* talk (and maybe bitch?) about our kids. And we laugh a lot at some of the ways we parented them. I mean, who nurses their kids until they are five years old? Not many people outside our group.

The conversations are lively and sobering. We still need each other to bounce ideas about helping our children through adult challenges they may be facing. We talk about our relationships and the challenges we have. And one thing we all realize? We still need our "recipe" to keep our sanity.

We love our kids no matter what they do, respect that their values may be different than ours, and trust their intuition is guiding them. Their decisions may be different than ours, and we coach each other to stay out of our kids' business—easier for some of us than others, but I won't mention any names.

At the end of the night, we raise our glasses in a toast to the friendships we have created, the children that we have parented, and the recipe that still guides us—as well as, we hope, our kids who are on their own with their own communities of kindred spirits.

*Initials and abbreviations used to respect the privacy of certain friends.

Editor's Side Dish

Cultural and Generational Flavor Distinctions

*"Your ability to shape your destiny is directly proportional to
your belief that it is a matter of will and determination—
however much or little that belief may be."*

- James A. Owen

One of the things that struck me when I first read—and even deeper as I edited—Patti's stories was the similarity between her relationship with Katie and my relationship with my mother. I noticed individual similarities between each of us, but especially how much I have in common with *both* Katie and Patti. I consider both of them friends, and I often empathize, relate, and understand *both* of their sides when they're having one of their patented "heated discussions."

As I was going through the edits in the "It Takes a Village" chapter, it struck me how generational differences— and the cultures that created those differences—play an important role in how parents define themselves, their responsibilities, and their relationship with their children. Each generation has a certain level of rebellion against their parents and their parents' culture. As Patti asks in several

places, what parent doesn't plan to do a better job than their parents did?

I ended up not having kids, but I absolutely believed I'd do a better job than my parents when I was thinking of having kids. (For the record, my parents were and are pretty awesome.) I clearly remember my dad taking time to explain why he said and did things because, he'd told us, he'd hated when his dad would say, "Because I'm your dad, and I said so!" (Not gonna lie: I absolutely tested his explanation limits. Just like I tested my parents' promise, "You can ask us about anything. If we don't know, we'll research it together." Also honestly: I'm super-proud of how my parents modeled being non-judgmental (I reallllllly explored "anything"), as well as willing to research even the most delicate topics. That experience made me a person I'm proud of, who others trust to help with difficult situations.)

When it comes to rebelling against social and parental "norms," the 60s—when Patti was in school and my parents were getting married—was when this behavior really exploded. While Patti is from the "Boomer" generation, she was born in the later half, which has several cultural distinctions from earlier Boomers. My mom was born at the end of the Post War generation, on the cusp of the Boomer generation—another period of transition and social change, which (I theorize) is why, despite she and my dad being "older" parents, they often skewed more liberal and nonconformist than my peers' parents. There are only nine years between Katie and me, so both our parental sets were raising children in this very different time from what they grew up in. Our parents were leaving prior generations' culture of "children should be seen, not heard, and contribute to society by doing what's expected of them" to a culture of "children should learn to think critically and contribute to society by making it better."

I was born in 1978—the tail end of Generation X or, according to some sources, part of the Xennial micro-generation. I best identify with this Xennial "cuspness" to Gen

X and Millennials. I'm drawn to transition and connectedness, but also distinction and transformation. Katie was born in 1987, smack in the central Millennial generation, and the socio-political culture Millennials were raised in.

My mother, Patti, Katie, and I are from four very different generations, but also, both Patti and my mother came into parenthood later, so there is an *extra* generation between them and their children—an extra changeover in cultural expectations.

In a later chapter—no spoilers, I promise—Patti had written a conversation she'd had with Peter regarding some questions I'd had on a story about how furious she'd been at the double standards for how men and women were treated in her Italian family when she was growing up and when her mom was growing up. The conversation didn't quite fit in that chapter, but I wanted to include it here:

> But now, as I [Patti] write this, my husband offered a different perspective. In my grandparent's generation, the roles for men and women were clearly defined. The man was the breadwinner and went off to work every day to provide for the family. The woman stayed home and tended to the sustenance of the family. Daughters were trained to take on their mothers' roles while sons followed suit with their dads'. Heck, my dad had started working when he was thirteen to help support the family while his older brother enlisted in the Army and went to college. It was a different time, a different generation, and a different culture.

> But even looking at these roles from my husband's perspective, it still appears to me that women had a lot more responsibilities than the men. Even through the nineties, if someone asked a stay-at-home mom if she "worked," she usually said "no." Of course she worked! She worked her ass off to take care of the kids and household

responsibilities. It was and still is a lot! Our generation worked hard to start changing that concept... And now we have dads staying home if moms' jobs are more lucrative.

I'd add that later generations also worked hard to not only change that concept, but broaden it so that people of color, people of different economic classes, and people who don't fit into traditional "man" or "woman" labels could have equal rights to live, work, and lovingly nourish their families. Looking specifically at the expectations, definitions, and perceptions of gender roles, there have been massive changes even just starting from Patti's generation through the current Generation Alpha (kids born starting in 2010).

And from each of those generations, you will absolutely meet equal rights activists who will argue up, down, and sideways about how the older or younger generation got it or is getting it *all wrong!* I truly believe most of these activists, regardless of generation, *do* come from places of love and a desire to end injustice. So why so much animosity?

We are all children of our generations.

Parents and their kids—all persons—are informed by the culture of their generation. Our relationship to intuition, our philosophy and beliefs, and how we understand and experience unconventional love—all of that develops as we grow up. Parents may be a child's ultimate teacher, but as they raise their children, parents are *also* affected by the world—from global issues to neighborhood changes—and how information about the world is shared. With each new generation, look at the growth in what information was available, how quickly it could be updated, and how easily it could be manipulated. Now consider how each generation of children is influenced by how they experience the world, and on top of that, they can compare their direct experience with the world to how they see their parents experience the same things.

Let's get back to those parent-child "heated discussions"—mothers and daughters in this case. Patti's recipe is for parents who want their kids to have better lives than they did. And even if they've had good lives, they want *better* for their kids. If their kids are to have better lives, then it follows that they need to do a better job parenting than their parents.

Kids are little sponges that absorb *everything*—whether their parents want them to or not—so they pick up on their parents' plans. Even if they don't end up parents themselves, they're instilled with the message they need to do *something* better than their parents. At least from my experience—and what I've observed from my mom, Patti, and Katie—that *something* is making the world better for future generations.

Except we *aren't* those future generations. We've grown up; the world of our formative years is gone, just like the world of our parents' formative years. We can only work with the information and experiences we've had.

But...

Awareness of those limitations, of how each of us are shaped by the world we grew up in, can be a guide to help us better tap into our intuition, inform our philosophy and beliefs, and come closer to *unconditional* in our acts of love.

Now to *remember* those important recipe modifications next time we're with our respective mothers or daughters...

Chapter Eight

Seasoning Affirmations:
Your Recipe Becomes What You Say It Is

"If you aren't making any mistakes,
it's a sure sign you're playing it too safe."

- John Maxwell

Believe it or not, sometimes your children really do listen to you! Of course, sometimes their attentiveness—proof that your version of the parenting recipe is working—doesn't go exactly as you think it will.

I'm not talking about that inevitable moment one of your kids repeats the F-bomb you drop, though don't beat yourself up when that happens either. It's not like they won't hear it eventually. I'm talking about how even your positive lessons have the potential to backfire and bite you in the ass.

"I will become what you say I am," at face value, would appear to be a very positive statement, right?

Let me tell you about *that* particular *Holy Shit*! lesson...

Katie and I clashed a lot during her teen years—

Who am I kidding? She's challenged me since she was born. (You read my earlier chapters, right?) I know that must sound so foreign to all moms with daughters reading this, right? No? Well, if it does, count your blessings!

On this particular day, Katie and I were having one of our "lively discussions." I can't even tell you what it was about now, but I can say I was not in my most resourceful state and my patience was wearing very thin.

Things had gotten to a point where I felt my best strategy was to ignore her, but she chased me down the hall, screaming, "Patricia, I am the mom and you are the daughter. You need to listen to *me!*"

That triggered me. I couldn't believe her disrespect! I shouted back, "You are so nasty!"

Katie was ready with a snarky, "I will become whatever you say I am."

Rather than turning around and smacking her (like my mother might have done), I was stopped in my tracks. My psyche shifted immediately. I realized, *Holy Shit! She actually listens to me.*

In the deluge of research Peter and I read prior to becoming parents (and more after Katie was born), we were drawn to strategies different from how we were brought up. Don't we all think we can do a better job than our parents? In my arrogance, I secretly wanted kids so I could parent them the way I wished I was parented.

One of those resources was Louise Hay.[4] (Thank you, Louise, for being a mentor for me!) Louise was and still lives in my mind and my heart as the queen of affirmations. The affirmation, "You will become what you say to yourself," was a biggie that always stood out for me, even before planning to become a parent.

During my awkward teenage years, I was always calling myself stupid and thinking about all the stupid things I did. I regularly berated myself for not being good enough, smart enough, thin enough...*perfect* enough.

I didn't want my kids to grow up with that model.

As you can imagine, Peter and I had to retrain our own brains to affirm the positive to ourselves first before we could teach our kids. We needed to be the example in word and action. As our kids grew up, we worked hard to embody this. If our kids berated themselves, if someone criticized our kids unconstructively—even if we overheard another parent speaking to their kid in a way that could break them down rather than affirm—Peter or I would step in and create a learning moment.

"Those kids will become whatever their parents keep telling them, and you will become whatever you tell yourself."

We'd make a point of explaining to our kids that some other parents didn't realize what they were saying, or they probably wouldn't say that to their kids. (As I'm writing this, it feels a little snooty to be so judgy of other parents, yet I believe if they could hear themselves, they might choose other ways to handle those challenging situations.)

Back to the *holy shit* of me, Katie, and her calling me out.

When she said, "I will become whatever you say I am," after I told her she was "nasty," I was proud of her! She got it!

What did I do in that moment of realization?

I was stunned. After a pause, I finally blurted, "Thank you, Katie. You're right…" I went on for a bit about how much I loved her and Christopher, and how she had just taught me a lesson. I don't remember the exact words from so long ago, but they seemed to be what she needed to hear. I asked, "May I give you a hug?"

She allowed the hug, and the day went on.

Part of a good family recipe is that it changes. When you share a recipe, especially a simple one, others are going to interpret the ingredients and steps to suit their needs. Sometimes *you* even forget the ingredients—even for your favorite recipe!—and someone else has to remind you what's missing. As a parent, your recipe for raising your children should yield well-developed persons with their own spirits, and there will come a time, probably sooner than you think, where they will teach you or remind you of the lessons you taught them. That you may have forgotten.

My butter and sage "Gavadeel" both is and is not my grandmother's "Gavadeel" with tomato sauce. And while I believe she would be proud I was using her lessons to nourish my family, she would probably be as enthused at my interpretation of it as I was with Katie throwing my own words back at me in that moment.

And if I'm being *entirely* honest, if she were to pop up as a ghost and tell me what she thought of my interpretation of her pasta recipe, I *might* be every bit as snarky as my daughter.

***

I vowed I would never be like my parents. And don't we all? At least to some extent?

My reasoning? Part was ego. I was certain I could do a better job than they did.

As I have said, I am a nonconformist at heart. I question the status quo, and my parents *were* the status quo.

"Just do it because I said so."

"You're too young to know any better."

"I'm the mother and that's that!"

Or worse,

"Wait until your father gets home!"

"I brought you into this world, and I can take you out!"

Sound familiar? Have your own list? I'm sure you do!

I certainly wasn't going to regurgitate words like that to *my* children! Certainly not!

Well, I tried. I made *every* effort to catch myself. But sometimes, especially in those especially heated situations...

If my husband was within earshot, he would comment (in the kindest way he could), "You sound a little like your mother."

No matter how kindly he tried, my Italian temper got triggered. But as much as I didn't like being called out and wanted to punch him, it was helpful to be reminded. So, I continued to find new ways and new words to use during challenging times. Some would say it's a lesson in futility. Maybe. Except there are those blessed moments when we can catch ourselves. And then it is a moment of pure ecstasy.

So, yes, I was determined to do a "better" job than my parents.

But if I'm being *really* honest—and that's my goal for this book— my biggest reason for wanting to do things differently?

I wanted my kids to *like* me.

I wanted them to be inspired by me and open to learning from me. I wanted them to know I valued their perspective and that their feelings mattered.

I realize now that that these are all things I craved from my parents. And I don't blame them for not giving me all those things. They did their best with the knowledge, experiences, and influences of their parents and the generations of parents' influence before them.

I grew up in a classic, Italian-American home in the 1960s. Children were to be seen and not heard. Discipline was done a certain way, and moms didn't care if you didn't like their directives.

I can't tell you how many times my siblings and I fought, and if Mom caught us and punished us as she deemed appropriate, it wasn't abnormal for one of us to say, "You are so mean." (We would never think of doing that with our father, but that's a different story.)

And Mom's response would go something like, "Yes. I'm the meanest mom. But you are still doing..." (dishes, chores, going to our rooms, whatever.)

It was probably what many moms of that era said. We learned that it was okay to dislike our moms. They gave us permission to dislike them with their words.

I become what I say I am.

Fast forward to me sitting in my car with two kids who had fought all the way home from school and through all the errands we'd had run. Their shrill voices had all the hairs on the back of my arms standing on end. Even as I pulled into the driveway, they were *still* at it.

"That's it!" I yelled. "Up to your rooms! If you can't stop fighting, then you are grounded until dinner!"

"You're the meanest mom on the planet!" one of them yelled back.

The script from my childhood would have me say, "Yes I am, but you're still going up to your room."

Instead, a voice from deep inside me said not to accept that dialogue about myself. I caught myself before those words left my mouth. *I am not a mean mother,* I thought. *And I am certainly not the meanest mom on the planet!*

I took a breath, and by divine providence, I replied, "No, I'm not. I'm the best mom on the planet for both of you, and you'll repeat it after me!"

Christopher was first to repeat the mantra. "You're the best mom on the planet."

Katie, not wanting to give me the satisfaction, said, "Whatever he said."

That was a good enough start for me.

I'm the best mom on the planet wasn't just a response to my children; it was a gentle reminder for me. It was changing my programmed beliefs via self-talk.

I *am* the best mom for them. The universe chose me to carry them, birth them, love them, protect them, and nurture them until they could take on the world themselves. I am the best mom for them, and I wasn't having anyone in my house say otherwise.

That moment of divine inspiration—*intuition*, if you will—empowered me. It educated me. It became a mantra whenever I would second guess a decision or when I was struggling with some new parenting challenge. When mommy-guilt or insecurity weighed me down (and let's face it, that happens!), those words reminded me that no one loves my kids quite like I do. I could pull my shoulders back and think, "Yeah, Patti! You've got this!"

And *holy shit,* I'm right!

How do I know I did a good job teaching my children positive mantras that honored me?

Several years ago, I was speaking to an audience of about four hundred chiropractors, their staff, and their families. My husband and children were also in the audience. I shared how I "programmed" my children to think I was the greatest mom on the planet by saying it to them and having them repeat it over and over for the first ten or so years of their life. I did it so much that all I would have to say to them is, "why did I do that?" to which they would reply—sometimes in a joking or mocking way (which was so cute!)—"because you're the best mom on the planet."

After the talk, I was approached by several attendees asking me about parenting, and out of the corner of my eye, I noticed my son standing off to the side, alone and watching me.

My first thought was, *Oh shit! He found out my secret!*

As soon as I had a free moment, I walked over to him and sheepishly said, "Christopher, I am so sorry that you had to hear how I programmed you and Katie in front of all these people."

Without hesitation, he replied, "That's okay, Mom." He paused with a little smirk. "You know why, Mom?"

"Whyyy?" I asked cautiously.

"Because you ARE the most wonderful mom on the planet."

Excuse me. I *still* need to grab some tissues...

Okay, now that I've had my moment, you may ask, "Patti, how do I do that with my kids?"

The answer? Just do it! Steal my lines; I give you permission. Fake it 'til you make it.

I grabbed these moments and acknowledged them to myself. You might need to write it down or find a way to embed it into your consciousness. Do whatever you need. Use moments like this to affirm things about yourself.

These are a few more of mine:

"I'm the perfect mom for my kids!"

"I am an awesome chiropractor!"

"I am stronger than I thought I was!"

"I have patience and pause before saying something I will regret!"

"I have the greatest husband on the planet!"

"I have the most wonderful kids on the planet!"

"I am an amazing cook!"

And you absolutely have my permission to start telling your children you are the best parent on the planet, and I will not be offended because you *are* the best parent on the planet *for them*, as I am for mine. We can start a club and invite *more* parents to join.

Affirmations are important because they clarify who you are and let you parent out of a place of strength and clarity. They are those "secret ingredients" that you and only you can add to the recipe. Try it, and see how it goes for you.

My parenting recipe only shows you the basics of following your heart, having clarity of your values, and listening to your intuition. You get to add your own spice to it to make it your own.

This picture of Katie (4 years old) and Christopher (2 years old) says it all about their personalities.

Coffee Break

A Lesson in the Weeds

*"Having a soft heart in a cruel world
is courage, not weakness."*

- Katherine Henson

In the vein of our children being little sponges, absorbing our words, thoughts, actions, and then spitting them back out when we least expect it, I want to share an entirely different *holy shit* moment and lesson given to me by Christopher.

When he was two and Katie was four, we were getting ready to move into a brand-new home office!

For nine months beforehand, while Peter worked our chiropractic practice, Christopher, Katie, and I were in charge of overseeing the development and building. The previous owners had created a Christmas tree farm, and hundreds of adorable evergreens about a foot tall would have been buried or lost as contractors dug our new foundation.

Devastated at that possibility, I enlisted Katie and Christopher in my mission to save the trees. "They could die if we don't take care of them!"

We manage to dig up and save twenty or more trees, replanting them when the contractors were done moving

dirt. We watered, cared for, and loved those little trees—and fortunately, they survived both the construction and the winter!

Come the following July, we met with our landscaper to discuss a nursery for cultivating plants before giving them a permanent home somewhere on the property, similar to what the kids and I did for the little Christmas trees. As Peter and I walked around the yard with her, Christopher waddled around with us while holding on to my pant leg.

It never dawned on me how hard he was listening or that he was even interested at all.

We chose a spot for the nursery, and the gardener explained, "I'll put the plastic down here. But we will need to leave it there for two weeks so that it kills all the weeds. We want them all dead before we can plant any trees for the nursery."

Peter and I agreed with her suggestions and left to play with Christopher in a different part of the yard while the landscaper spent the rest of the day prepping the selected nursery area.

The next morning, however, as I opened the back door to the yard, Christopher just about flew out. He raced straight past me, as fast as his toddler legs could carry him, and headed to the nursery area. When he got there, he frantically started pulling up the plastic.

That little imp! I thought to myself. *What is he doing, wrecking all the landscaper's work?* I opened my mouth to yell at him—

And stopped.

What *was* he doing wrecking all our hard work? That wasn't like him at all. Christopher was not a destructive child. There was obviously something going on in his little head if I could take the time to figure it out. So I got down on my knees real close to him, gently put my hand on his back, and asked, "What are you doing, Christopher?"

He turned to look at me, big brown eyes filled with concern. "I don't want the weeds to die!"

My heart melted. "What do you mean?"

"Mommy, you told me it's not nice to kill things. I don't want to kill the weeds. I don't want them to die."

I tell you, the tears welled up in my eyes at that moment.

Had we not just spent months of time and energy making sure those Christmas trees didn't die? How would he know that weeds are different from evergreens? He was only two!

And really, are they so different?

"Oh, you're right, Christopher! It's not nice to kill things! We won't kill the weeds!" I hugged him and said, "Let's save the weeds."

For the next fifteen minutes, we dramatically tore up all the plastic.

That was over thirty years ago. We never did get our nursery. But every spring, I look out of my window at a patch of wildflowers where it should have been. They are beautiful. People might call them weeds, but to me, they are a little symbol of freedom, kindness, and the power of being congruent and teaching your children your values.

If I hadn't taken the time to ask, I would have reacted as if he were naughty. He would have felt the shame and the guilt of my reaction. Instead, he'd reflected back what I'd taught him: It's not nice to kill or bring harm to things. That's not who we are.

In living my philosophy and values, in showing unconditional love, and in trusting my intuition, I had made a space for this child to grow into a caring being who lived true to the values he'd been taught.

Believe it or not, your kids *are* listening to you.

And believe it or not, a simple recipe *can* nourish a family in many surprising ways.

Chapter Nine

A Recipe, Not a Box: Feeding Young Minds (Education Part 1)

"Education is the passport to the future, for tomorrow belongs to those who prepare for it today."

\- Malcolm X

If you couldn't tell by now, Peter and I don't navigate the world like most do. We are "think outside of the box" kind of people, so it should be no surprise that when it was time for our kids to go to school, we were very picky about their education.

Some of the parents we knew took the route of home schooling, and in recent years, the options for parents who want to take that journey have grown immensely. This is where building a good community and team can help a lot. Learning what resources are in your area and what is involved in home schooling is necessary to make the best decision for you and your children.

As for me, based on my research and knowing myself, I was not cut out to home school.

Hey, is that philosophy (research, collecting all the data I can), unconditional love (for myself and my children), and intuition at work or what?

In fact, applying this recipe was critical throughout the entire journey of our children's education—for our health as parents as well as for our kids' futures. Like with every part of parenting, sometimes it was surprisingly easy to do this.

Other times it was not.

Let me serve you a bit of a "tasting menu" of some lessons in our journey...

***

Right from the start, Peter and I agreed our children should experience more of the world earlier in life. I'd been raised in a mostly Italian neighborhood in Newark, NJ, with very few people of color around us, and Peter grew up similarly in Brighton, MA. We valued our children interacting with kids of different cultures, and unfortunately at the time, our town did not provide that environment.

One of our best friends referred us to the Hollow Reed School, a multiracial school in Boston that covered preschool to second grade. Their child, a few years older than ours, raved about the experience of community, safety, and creativity. Even better, our educational philosophy (similar to Montessori schools[5]) aligned with Hollow Reed letting children be free to learn through play in a stimulating environment with art, music, and dance.

Katie fit right in at the Hollow Reed School. She was loved and accepted unconditionally by the staff. Yet it wasn't without challenges. For example, Katie was hypersensitive to touch and had night terrors, waking up from naps screaming but not wanting physical contact. We informed the school when she started, so they were aware of this when Katie inevitably had episodes during scheduled naptimes. Faculty and staff worked with our schedule to avoid Katie napping at the school and offered counseling. By her second year, the night terrors stopped. Katie was able to have a positive and safe environment for her first worldly experience while Peter and I had peace of mind knowing she was cared for by kindred spirits who understood her challenges and helped her grow.

Christopher joined Katie at Hollow Reed School when he was almost four and would have a similar, life-enriching experience. He met a boy named Ben by biting him while they were both outside playing.

That's not the whole story, but if the school hadn't handled this incident the way they did, this story could have had a much worse ending.

Once again, in true form, the faculty and staff made choices that empowered the students (Christopher and Ben in this instance) and their families. They called a meeting with both sets of parents and mediated a discussion to find out what happened and what was at the root of the behavior.

When we met Ben's parents, we found like-minded compatriots. Our conversation, which included both boys, revealed that Ben had bitten Christopher first over some disagreement, and Christopher had responded in kind.

"Kids can just be kids," was their feeling. "Let's use this as a teaching moment for both of them."

We did, and to this day, Christopher and Ben are best friends while Peter and I still maintain our friendship with Ben's parents.

As for knowing how this could have been a sadder outcome without the school's efforts to create a productive space for communication and mediation, a similar incident happened months later. Christopher had bitten another student under circumstances we never fully got to learn. That student's parents were brought in for a similar conversation.

And it did *not* go so well.

These parents were livid and not open to any conversation. They wanted to sue us, sue the school, and they demanded Christopher's immediate expulsion. Ben's parents even came in to speak on ours and Christopher's behalf, but the parents would not listen to any reason. The parents eventually pulled their child from the school without any litigation; they were not a good fit for the environment the school was creating. But if not for the faculty and staff creating space for communication, exploring the full situation, and not making assumptions about any child, it could have turned out a lot messier.

***

You know deep within your intuitive soul what your children and your family need. Your intuitive soul knows who they are, what they want, and what is needed to empower them to the next level. That being said, this *knowing* requires tuning in to your kids from the moment you connect—whether it's a sense you get when they are growing inside you or when you first meet them—and it doesn't stop no matter how old they get. It requires really listening to their cues and responding from your heart.

Another early and important lesson for Peter and me was realizing we needed to adjust our strategies and expectations for two *very different* learners.

While Katie bloomed in many ways during those first few educational years, she was six and not reading while her four-year-old brother was starting to read. Even before that, we observed many things just came easier for Christopher. He started walking at nine months old and was speaking in full sentences by two, whereas Katie didn't start walking until she was fifteen months, and she learned to speak in full sentences from communicating with her brother.

And that affected their relationship as siblings. While Katie often looked up to her little brother with admiration—and eagerly learned from him—she was also frustrated that she didn't grasp things as quickly as he did.

Back to my recipe to ensure the most nourishing education for *both* of our children!

After continued research on educational theories (our philosophy) and seeing where each of our children thrived and were challenged (unconditional love and intuition), we looked for more structured learning experiences beyond the Hollow Reed School.

One of our chiropractic patients was the head of admissions at a particular private school—and there's community stepping up!—invited Katie to spend a day to see how she integrated with the other kids in the classroom. I dropped Katie off and was told by this woman, who we'll call "Jane" to protect the innocent, that I could pick her up at two in the afternoon.

Katie cried and didn't want me to leave her. She'd cried when I'd first left her at Hollow Reed School too, and let me tell you, it wasn't *any* easier the second time around. I drove home worried that I was a terrible parent, and worse, *guilty*—because I also felt *relieved* that someone else was watching my child while I returned to my fulfilling job, the pleasure of being in my practice, the vocation I was called to.

Two o'clock finally rolled around, and I joined several other parents arriving to pick up our kids. I found Katie in the classroom, quietly playing with some kids in the corner. Everything looked good!

She'd been all right without me!

That relief and joy was short-lived. Jane pulled me aside with a frown and informed me, "I don't think our school is the right fit for Katie."

My stomach sank. I glanced back to Katie, who looked like she was fitting in fine. But something in Jane's tone raised my protective mama hackles. "Why not?"

"Well, we don't allow our children to pick up chairs and try to throw them at other children."

"Excuse me?" I waited for some explanation. I knew with all my heart Katie wouldn't just *attack* another child. With her sensitivity, if someone had tried to touch or grab her, even innocently, that might have caused her to act up—but not to *that* degree!

The woman went on describe how Katie had made a huge emotional scene and scared all the other kids.

When she was done, I was furious, but managed to cordially ask, "And what caused this emotional upset? Katie is a kind person, so something must have provoked her."

"It doesn't matter. We can't allow her to join our class. Perhaps you should have your daughter tested, get a core evaluation to determine the right kind of school for her."

I wanted to inform the woman that it *did* matter, and it *should* matter for any child attending the school. But my intuition said that this *school* was not a good fit for our family and our values. If this woman had this reaction to Katie and wasn't willing to listen, and *Katie* had had such a reaction in this environment, I shouldn't waste my time convincing them otherwise.

I brought Katie home. We would find the right educational environment for her. This just wasn't the one.

***

For much of Katie's early life, many well-intentioned friends, family, and teachers encouraged us to have her tested to see what she "had" that made her different. Even today, we're far from alone in getting this kind of parental advice, whether or not we solicit it.

Now, we knew Katie was unique and had some challenges. Christopher had his quirks too. Don't we all? We wanted our children to be programmed toward health and potential, not toward limitations and disorders. But while we didn't want Katie to be officially labeled, we needed more information to give her the best possible emotional, physical, spiritual, and intellectual input to allow her to reach the fullest potential of who she could be. Just as we wanted for Christopher.

Part of our philosophy is if you are going to get tested for something, it's a good idea to know ahead of time what the possible recommendations would be. Then you would have the option to embark upon the recommendations and forego the diagnosis. And that is what we did.

We enlisted a member of our practice who was an expert in the field of neurodiversity (not a term commonly used at the time) to do an "unofficial" assessment of Katie's cognitive development. She gave us information and tools to support Katie in her neurological growth, and those same tools would be accessible to Christopher as well. We loved it because it didn't single Katie out as having deficiencies that needed to be fixed. It allowed us to see both our children's individual challenges and strengths so we could focus on building their strengths and supporting their challenges.

It was similar to if you had one child who needed a special diet for their body, but that diet is, overall, one that promotes health to most bodies. Both our kids would benefit. Researching and finding more unorthodox (particularly at that time) tools to address our children's different learning needs not only helped with their cognitive development, but it cultivated a close bond between them that remains today.

But we still needed to find the right school for our children after their time at Hollow Reed.

Peter and I needed more data, so in addition to our diagnostic testing and newfound tools, we decided to get a more traditional core evaluation. Katie's results showed that she wouldn't do well in a special needs school or classroom. She'd be best served in a private school with a small student-to-teacher ratio.

Armed with all the information we could obtain, we pushed forward in our school search. Once again, our community was there to help.

***

Two families in our practice had children that didn't "fit in" at public schools. Their kids had been given labels, had Individual Education Plans (IEPs), and were treated as outcasts by their peers, teased and bullied horribly. They were miserable, so their parents had embarked on a similar search for a better education for their children's needs. And they'd found it.

Delphi Academy provided a learning environment where their children were happy, learning, and making friends. The school also had a much more diverse population than many other private schools. While these families, and ours, were able to pay the tuition—and easily justified the expense because it was the answer to our families' and kids' sanity and health—the school also offered financial aid and assistance, which was how they could serve students from a variety of backgrounds.

The Delphi Academy philosophy is to not label children. They were, just like at Hollow Reed School and just like we wanted, giving each child what they needed intellectually, emotionally, and physically based on each child's individual learning style and cognitive capabilities. They used their own assessment tools and determined each child's independent program, similar to a public-school IEP. The school promoted ethics and leadership skills along with reading, writing and math, and they allotted two hours during the school day for physical activity. *Holy shit!* Two hours of physical education would be awesome for our kids! With a student-to-teacher ratio of ten to one, the school taught children "how to learn" independently. The system of learning, called "study technology," was used in this school and in six other Delphian schools in the U.S. at that time.

Katie and Christopher could each learn at their own pace and not be in competition!

All that, and it was less than ten miles (about a half-hour's drive) from our home. It was almost too good to be true. *Holy shit!* Our efforts and work had found an answer that fit our family!

Katie and Christopher spent the next couple years thriving at Delphi. But when Christopher was going to pass Katie's academic level, we knew it was time to find a new school for Katie. Thus began the next part of our journey in education, with new challenges to—

and further proof of—the recipe of philosophy, intuition, and unconditional love being a trustworthy parenting recipe.

***

I grew up in a blue-collar family. We rarely (if ever) went out to eat, and we bought our clothes from discount stores. My parents were concerned about where to send us girls to high school. Unbeknownst to me until my sister recently informed me, a large percentage of girls in our public high school were getting pregnant, so my parents wanted us girls to go to Catholic school. My dad's salary, alone, couldn't afford that, so my mom went to work full-time (unusual for their generation) so that when their oldest girl was ready for high school, they could afford the private tuition.

For me to naively say that when you value something enough, you find the means to make it happen would be very insensitive. Let's face it, private school tuitions have skyrocketed since I was in high school.

For our own reasons, Peter and I valued the benefits of finding a private school for our children. It was already established that Katie would not thrive in a public school's special education class. We researched vouchers from the state and our town to help us pay, hoping we would get some type of assistance. When we realized we would need to pay for tuition, we put a lot of effort to create a lucrative and successful chiropractic practice that allowed us to afford private school for both our kids. Had we not been able to meet that cost, we would have advocated for assistance and accommodations from the public school for Katie.

You might be saying, "Well, you had the means to do all these things for your kids, what can *I* do in *my* financial/work/family/living situation? I don't have those choices."

I get that. I do. The choices I made and was able to make are the best choices I could make in my situation; you need to make the best choices in your situation.

A close friend of ours, whose children were born deaf, needed to advocate for her kids to get the right help at school. She wanted her kids to be mainstreamed and needed an aide to be with her kids while in the classroom. Even though she was an introvert, she found her voice to speak up at school meetings and fight for greater accessibility. She was successful, and her kids—and likely others—were able to receive the help they needed.

You could be in a similar or even better economic situation than I was, and my choices still might not be the best ones for your families. I share my story as one example of how you can use the adaptable recipe of philosophy, intuition, and unconditional love to help your children better thrive in their education.

What is it you believe in? What is your philosophy? How does it apply to your children's educational path?

What does your gut tell you your children need? What are the insightful whispers from that little voice in your heart that no one— no teacher, no doctor, no administrator—can hear but you? How does your heart feel about your choices?

With your knowledge, your means, and your ability, what choices do you have that show the most love to your children? How can you educate yourself to be the best advocate for their learning?

We have more resources now than I had in the 80s and 90s. There are more programs for home schooling and alternative schools. Even among those I mention, such as Delphi Academy, there are programs for financial aid, as well as transportation and housing for those outside the area.

Even the tools have gotten better over the years. I recently had the opportunity to see new, mind-blowing programs, such as The Spellers Method™ [6] for non-verbal autistic kids that allowed them to spell out words and communicate with their parents for the first time in their lives. And there are more online programs, apps, and games made for students whose brains function in ways that don't fit in with traditional schooling.

Check the internet, visit local libraries, and consult your community. Use these tools to hone your philosophy, open opportunities for your intuition to direct you, and unconditionally love your children by ensuring they learn what they need to be their best selves.

Coffee Break

Touch, Consent, and Honoring the Body

*"I have always tried to keep my integrity
and keep my autonomy."*

- Annie Lennox

I mentioned that I changed my grandmother's "Gadaveel" recipe because my recipe needed to respect my body's needs. As your family grows, you'll find each of their bodies will have particular needs, and your recipe should honor those.

One of Katie's lessons for us was her sensitivity to touch, so our parenting recipe needed to accommodate that—and empower her to care for those needs as she grew older.

When I was a child, I grew up in a time where if an adult asked for a hug, kiss, or other affection, you did what you were told and gave them that affection. No matter how you felt. No matter how uncomfortable that adult made you. I hated that as a child. Without naming particular people, there were some adults who I *had* to hug or *had* to kiss that did things they shouldn't have to a young girl.

Even before knowing Katie's needs, I'd decided I would not subject my children to forced affection and touch. I would teach them they had power and control over their bodies.

They were allowed to say "no" to anyone touching them without their consent.

I'm happy more and more parents are now teaching their children (and families) this kind of bodily autonomy, but let me tell you, when Peter and I told friends and family members they could *not* hug, kiss, or touch Katie or Christopher unless that child said they could... Well, it caused more than a few waves.

But we stood by this decision and still do. Our children get to make their own choices about what happens to their bodies. And they know to ask others' consent before touching them.

Chapter Ten

A Recipe, Not a Box: Engineering School Lunch Plans (Education Part 2)

*"Education is not something which the
teacher does, but a natural process that develops spontaneously
in the human being."*

\- Maria Montessori

A priority Peter and I shared was that we wanted our children to know they held answers inside of them, and we held true to those beliefs time and again. We wanted to imprint positive affirmations and teach them about how to make decisions starting at an early age.

If they were sick with a cold, we would tell them, "You have a smart body, a healthy body. Your body knows how to heal you." And they healed, learning this was true.

In times when they felt something was off with a person and they didn't want to speak with them or get a hug, we would acknowledge that: "I'm so proud you knew not to talk to that person because Mommy got a funny feeling from them too. It's important to listen to what you are feeling."

So when Katie was eleven and we realized she needed a different learning environment from Delphi Academy, where her younger brother had surpassed her in learning, we told her she would choose which school felt right for her. Giving her that decision empowered her, and she knew we would support her.

It was a month-long journey. She and I would make appointments with the different schools and talk about the experience. We visited our town public school and many private schools within thirty minutes of our home.

After visiting the last school on our list, I vividly remember sitting in the car in our driveway and asking Katie what she thought. I knew she'd give me her honest and unfiltered opinion, a trait I appreciate in her (usually). Her response was illuminating.

"You know, Mom, those private schools are pretty much the same as the public school, except you will pay a lot of money for me to go there. And I don't like any of them! I don't feel like I would fit in. I really want to find a school that is different. A school where the kids are different, and I will fit in because I am different."

Another *Holy shit!* moment. My eleven-year-old, neurospicy daughter was dropping serious insight. We were doing a good job parenting!

We continued our search.

Finally, we found Sudbury Valley School, which was twenty miles (forty-five minutes to an hour) away from our house—and in the opposite direction of Delphi Academy, where Christopher would be staying, which was half an hour away. In case you don't want to do the math, that was over two hours a day of driving (about 170 miles a day total), five days a week. We would make the sacrifice so our kids were in the best places for their emotional, physical, and intellectual growth. That's how strongly Peter and I felt about the environments we wanted for our children.

Sudbury Valley School was as unique as Katie; it was a fertile ground for her to learn social skills and find her passion for learning. The school's philosophy, which has been adopted by educational institutions across the United States, as well as in Australia, Belgium, Canada, France, Germany, Israel, Japan, and Switzerland, was to allow children to create their own learning process and utilize the tools made available at the school. They could play all day if they wanted or they could go to classes. All the courses taught were initiated by the students. Upon democratically deciding upon the course, they would approach the faculty and staff to find the teacher who was best suited to teach that particular subject.

It was an excellent atmosphere for children who did not "fit in" and were not thriving at a regular school (public or private). Every week the entire school (faculty, staff, and students) convened for a general meeting to discuss how the school would allocate its tuition assets, including discussion about salaries for all the employees, equipment that needed to be purchased, or how much toilet paper was in stock. Everything was done in a democratic process with the students, no matter what age, having a say in the decisions. In order to graduate, they needed to be there for three years minimum and write a thesis about how they would contribute to the community when they graduated.

Holy shit! What a concept!

It was mind-blowing to be part of such a learning situation. From the moment she stepped on the campus, Katie knew she would be happy. She was thrilled to find this place! During her time at Sudbury Valley, Katie was motivated to teach herself how to do magic tricks and become proficient in the art of creating balloon animals. For years, these were sources of income for her, and she still practices and teaches these skills for family and friends. In a typical school situation, she wouldn't be able to create this curriculum for herself, nor would she have been given the resources and support to turn it into a viable entrepreneurship.

Katie spent three blessed years at Sudbury Valley, and after her 2001 school year, little did any of us know, our family was in for our biggest change yet.

And I was in for an emotional rollercoaster.

Christopher was graduating from his last year at Delphi Academy. He'd been an excellent student, earning the highest honors in mathematics—surpassing any other student before him at the time! Upon his graduation, Delphian School in Oregon, mothership school to Delphi Academy, sent a recruiter to invite him to finish his education there.

Now, sending my kid to the other side of the country was not something I was ready for, but Christopher was excited about the opportunity.

As a compromise, we agreed he and Katie could attend the Delphian School summer camp that year while Peter and I traveled to

Italy together for the first time. I, for one, was *certain* after spending time away from us, my children would realize how much they missed their awesome parents and reject *any* plans for leaving home early. At least until college.

I was wrong.

Way wrong.

Both Christopher and Katie had fantastic experiences at the camp.

What I was expecting even less, though, was one of the school representatives reaching out to me about how the school could offer a learning experience for *Katie* that was tailor-made to her needs, including one-on-one support that would get her to a level of academic excellence.

Well, shit! If that wasn't music to my ears.

But *Oregon?*

My initial reaction was to laugh and say, "That's a bit far to commute every day from Boston."

Reality set in: On one hand, this was a fantastic opportunity for Katie that she wouldn't get near home. On the other hand, *my little girl was going to leave me!*

And then, of course, there was Christopher, who'd wanted to go since he'd been offered the opportunity. He'd already shown that he could excel in the Delphian environment. Why wouldn't we want him to continue with that?

All I could think was *my kids are going to leave me!*

Holy shit! Was I going to be an empty-nester long before I expected?

Was I being selfish? I wasn't ready to let go of my children. I wasn't done being their parent. I held onto my "long commute from Boston" joke for a while as a coping and avoidance mechanism. Funny right?

Then I called my friend and life coach, Jay, and told her that Katie wanted to go to school in Oregon.

"Hallelujah!" she screamed. "Did you buy the plane ticket yet?"

As you might have gathered if you've gotten this far in the book, Katie and I were each other's greatest antagonizers more often than not. We'd gotten really good at pushing each other's buttons. I'm sure absolutely *no other* mother of a teenaged daughter *ever* had secret fantasies of shipping their little girl across the country, right?

Not that we'd ever admit it, of course.

At Jay's response, I was mortified. And guilty. I'd also felt relief at this opportunity. *At this point in our lives,* I was thinking, *Katie and I might do well with a break from each other.*

On many levels, I couldn't imagine what life would be like without Katie. Or Christopher. The Delphian School in Oregon would be a place both our children would thrive, but I wasn't ready. Letting both of them go, all at once, might have broken me.

One of the many things Peter and I wanted for our children was that they honored their feelings and their needs. What lesson was I teaching if I didn't do the same for myself?

Of our two children, Katie *needed* the environment at Delphian School to not just excel, but simply perform at the levels necessary to graduate high school. (And excel, she did! When she graduated from the Delphian school and took her GED, she passed the first time around with a better than average score.) Christopher, I knew, had the type of mind that could do well in a variety of learning environments. I had to ask him to wait. For me.

The initial conversation didn't go great. I was honest and told him, "Christopher, I don't know what I'd do if I felt like I was losing both of you."

Christopher argued, logically and rationally, that he'd heard about more traditional schools and didn't think that he would be able to accomplish as much or excel as much in that kind of environment.

I offered other arguments. "You'd finally get the full attention of both your parents for the first time. Wouldn't that be nice? Don't you want to at least have the experience of another learning method so you know for certain what works for you? And you could carry that experience with you if go to Delphian School later."

I cried more than a few times, as much as I hated doing so. But I was desperate. To be my authentic self, I had to share that vulnerability. Was it selfish? Maybe. But it also showed my kids that *all* of us were allowed to be vulnerable. All of us, even me, were allowed to ask for help and allowed to ask others make reasonable concessions for our well-being. It was an act of unconditional love for myself—something a lot of parents forget they deserve too.

I can't tell you which was harder, imagining both kids leaving or asking to *receive* the kind of love I so readily gave.

Eventually, we reached a compromise. Katie would begin the school year in Oregon, and Christopher would remain home for one year and try a more traditional school. If he hated it, he could transfer to Delphian. And like we'd done with Katie, we let Christopher choose what school he would attend while he was here.

I was so grateful and proud of Christopher for accepting the situation, being willing to take care of my needs, and exploring this route that would, ultimately, be useful to him in his life.

I remember the day I dropped Katie off at the Delphian School in Sheridan, Oregon. After getting her set up in her dorm room, it was time for the parents to leave. One of the teachers was taking me back to the airport. As we pulled down the school driveway, Katie came running after the car, screaming, "Don't leave me!"

Just like when I dropped her off at prior schools. And just like all those prior times, I too was crying my eyes out.

I told you it never gets any easier!

Thank goodness someone else was driving, telling me to "look straight ahead," and assuring me once I was out of sight, she'd be fine.

Also, God bless every teacher, babysitter, and caretaker who has this duty of herding parents away so their children can have these lessons of independence.

Letting go is hard. Even if it means getting some long-needed freedom. For everyone.

Let go.

I'd had to "let go" so many times already, and it was always hard!

The ultimate letting go was giving birth and not having them in the safe confines of my body. And then the first time I let someone other than a family member hold them while I watched. When we left them home with a relative so Peter and I could go out on a much-needed date. The first time I hired a babysitter while Peter and I worked downstairs in the office. Every first day of school I had to drop them off...

I can still feel the angst in my body as I write about it.

And leaving my daughter *three thousand* miles away?

Holy shit! What was I thinking?

Within three to four weeks, Katie had adapted.

And so had I (somewhat). I still couldn't go in her room for weeks without crying. My baby was away from the nest with no one to protect her and take care of her like Mom.

As hard as it was for me to let her go, my gut knew it was the best choice and a blessing for both of us. Within those first couple of weeks, she would call me on the phone (at 1:00 AM Eastern Time) and cry, "No one understands me like you, and no one treats me as nice as you."

Those were the most beautiful sounds I'd heard from her since her first cry as a baby. With all the trials and tribulations we'd had, she loved and respected me. Because of her leaving the safety of our home, our relationship evolved to the next level.

Holy shit! Proof I *really* was the best mom on the planet for her!

A few months into Katie's time away, a friend of mine said that she had never seen me look so calm and relaxed in all the years she had known me. Sometimes you adapt without even knowing you are doing it! With all our challenges, Katie has been one of my greatest cheerleaders and my greatest teacher.

And while Katie was away, an evolution was occurring with Christopher—and with our relationship to Christopher.

We enrolled Christopher at St. Sebastian's, a Catholic high school close to our home that Peter had graduated from. It had an exceptional academic program, and Christopher maintained his excellent grades while he attended.

Christopher had stayed home for me, but also, I was right. His staying home that first year with Katie gone was a blessing for *all* of us, including Katie, who needed time away from the whole family to find her true self. It wasn't just that I wasn't ready to let both my kids leave—which was true—but my heart had realized there was more.

As I'd promised, Christopher finally got his mom's and dad's energy all to himself.

Peter got to attend Christopher's tennis matches—tennis being a new sport Christopher started at St. Sebastian's—without having to work around two kids' schedules. The two also were able to spend more time playing chess and board games while talking about, well, things fathers and sons talk about. Without interruption.

I, a night owl to Peter's morning bird tendencies, could dedicate evenings to my son, which usually included dealing with schoolwork.

St. Sebastian's learning methods were very different from the independent learning Christopher was used to. He was frustrated at first, feeling like he could have learned so much more at Delphi, studying at his own pace and not at the whim of the teacher. However, he was also exposed to experiences he wouldn't have otherwise had—particularly non-linear or non-mathematical ideas.

At Delphi Academy, Christopher excelled in math, engineering, and computer work, so the school supported his advanced learning in those subjects and allowed him to spend minimal attention on language, arts, and in general, more abstract thinking. At St. Sebastian's, he struggled to work in subjects and on topics he felt were unnecessary for his future, which he saw to be in computer science. He had to explore the non-quantifiable values and principles of religion, philosophy, and literature, and that was hard for him.

While he certainly didn't enjoy learning things that didn't come easy, especially as he was doing so, that year at home was a lesson he needed about the importance of developing the whole self outside of one's comfort zone. It was also a chance for him to face things he wasn't naturally good at and experience the growth in overcoming those challenges.

It was also an opportunity for me to connect with my son on a different level. I'd helped Katie through many struggles, and as I faced these obstacles with Christopher, we bonded in a new way. In fact, I realized how much we had in common!

Where Katie would take her frustrations out on the world around her, Christopher would internally beat himself up. *What's wrong with me? Why can't I do this right? I'm so good at these things, so why are these other things so hard?*

Just like me.

He'd watched me face my struggles through the years and internalized how I handled them—for better or for worse. But that meant I could level with him on a different scale than Katie. And I could see, reflected in him, where my own coping strategies worked well...and not so well.

One of the particular challenges he hated were that students were required to write essays every night. Writing was not a strong suit for Christopher, so he and I stayed up many a night (sometimes until the wee hours of the morning) writing essays together. And I loved it! Because we had similar coping strategies when we were frustrated, I could treat him how I wanted someone to treat me. *And it worked!*

When Christopher would come to me saying, "I can't do this! I don't know how to do this," I would offer suggestions. He didn't necessarily *like* my suggestions or that I was giving him suggestions, but they'd set his mind to thinking about the problem rather than spiraling around the "I can't."

Our evening sessions would fall into a comfortable pattern. He'd come and talk to me about how he hated whatever he was working on, I'd offer some suggestions, and he'd disappear (sometimes grumpily) back to his room. Some time later, he'd return, continue our conversation—sometimes pointing out why, exactly, my prior suggestions were wrong—we'd talk even more, and he'd go back to his room. Rinse, repeat, over and over. Eventually he'd come back to me with a finished product or announce it was finished, and go to bed.

By the end of the year, he had mastered essay writing, and I felt my help was a great contribution to his success.

Despite the positive growth in our family relationships, Christopher was also right: the traditional school model was not the best thing for him. He would transfer to the Delphian School the following year. I cherished those precious moments we had together and watched my son blossom emotionally, physically, and intellectually despite his desire to be in Oregon.

It was the toughest decision of Peter's and my life to let our children leave the nest at fifteen years old, but we knew intuitively we had to let them follow their dream. When people ask me why I sent my kids to a boarding school, I tell them that if Delphian was in Massachusetts, they would not have left home. Because Delphian had a similar philosophy to us regarding life, health, and education, it was a home away from home for our kids. We knew in our hearts that even across the country, our children would be safe, loved, and respected by the school's teachers and staff. They would be nurtured and nourished in body, mind, and spirit.

Each of us has a responsibility to ourselves to be our true self when we make important decisions about our lives and the impact it will have on our children—as a model to our children as well as for their benefit. It is so important to explore our philosophy and values because it is our philosophy and values that guide us in the day-to-day decisions as well as those moments when we need to make the tough decisions. In our journey to help our children get the best education for themselves, we had to learn about *learning*: how does one learn? How can one person learn differently than another?

While I wouldn't say our philosophy changed—we always wanted to make sure our children had the best education to become their best selves—it *expanded* with our knowledge base. And as we observed how different learning styles worked for each of our kids, our ability to help others find the right education options for *their* children using our shared philosophy was enhanced and strengthened.

As I look back at all the educational institutions our children attended from pre-school through their high school years, we were so blessed to have always found the perfect school at the perfect time. We did a hell of a lot of research—and driving, rearranging schedules, and being present advocates for our children—but every step of the way, we were guided by our philosophy, intuition, and the love for our children, each other, and ourselves.

These souls come to us for our safekeeping; each parent has their own spin on what a good outcome looks like based on their values, principles, and philosophy. Each family has their own situation, needs, and challenges they need to consider. Just like my grandmother's Gavadeel recipe, you have to know what *feels* right and makes the most sense. I adapted my grandmother's recipe, and I encourage you to do the same. If it doesn't fit your family, you don't have to do it my way—and shouldn't! Adapt your parenting recipe for your own children's educational needs. Listen to your heart, get good data, and follow your gut.

Editor's Side Dish:

Neurospicy Label Considerations

*"Neuroanatomy isn't destiny. Neither is genetics.
They don't define who you will be. But they do define
who you might be. They define who you can be."*

- Temple Grandin, *The Autistic Brain: Thinking
Across the Spectrum*

Neurospicy, adj. – A term created to promote inclusivity while referencing people whose brains work differently from what society considers "normal" or "typical."[7]

I mentioned in my earlier editorial "Side Dish" about generations how, as a friend to both Patti and Katie, I often see both sides of "heated discussions." Even before I started helping Patti with her book, one of the discussions that would come up with both of them, individually and together, was about "labeling" particular neurodiverse functionalities (what many still call or diagnose, for better or worse, as mental "disabilities").

I may have also mentioned (if it's not apparent from my writing voice) that I have ADHD, attention deficit hyperactivity disorder (the accuracy of the name is hotly

debated amongst professionals).[8] I was diagnosed, officially, almost ten years ago when my body was going through multiple hormone-related changes, perimenopause (if you have a doctor that believes perimenopause is a "thing") among them. This diagnosis led to the discovery and (blessedly) appropriate treatment of a variety of other issues. I was fortunate enough to have a therapist who shared the philosophy of doing as much research as possible. Also, fortunately, I'd gotten to a point in my relationship with my primary care doctor that she trusted my research ability, and we could have informed conversations about different treatments.

For me, ten years ago, having a "label" for my condition was life-changing. I learned ADHD brains process sugar differently than non-ADHD brains, which was why when I tried a fully ketogenic diet, my short-term memory and my focus became horrendous! And then got worse if, in emotional frustration, I indulged in a processed sugary treat —and nothing else. I needed a certain, steady level of accessible carbohydrates. Also, most ADHD brains don't have the ability to tell a person they are "full" until their stomach *feels* full—and is therefore *over*full. Once I got on the right medication for my ADHD (and that can vary, person to person), I lost the most weight than I *ever* had in my entire life (a life where, even as a baby, I was overweight). Without "dieting" specifically, I found dietary changes—the kind you can stick with for life—that also helped my brain's functionality. There's a reason study after study dependably finds massive overlaps in undiagnosed ADHD, obesity, and eating disorders![9]

Besides giving me (and my doctors) insights to some of the medical mysteries of my body, the ADHD diagnosis also was an emotional relief. I better understood why I was the way I was, why I didn't think like other people, why "normal" organizational tools never worked for me, and why I'd fall into unhealthy procrastination-cramming schedules. I learned I needed a different tool and skill set to accomplish the dreams I was passionate about.

Furthermore, in sharing my diagnosis, I inspired many of my friends—particularly women near my age—to more deeply explore their mental health because we shared a lot of symptoms. And then, in getting their various diagnoses, they were better able to address physical health issues that doctors hadn't been able to figure out. Now, many of these women hadn't been diagnosed (or diagnosed correctly) with ADHD (or autism spectrum disorder (ASD), the most currently accepted term among the autistic population) because the symptoms of these particular conditions can signify multiple issues and there is serious gender-bias in medical studies regarding these conditions. The combination of these factors lead to women not being diagnosed or not being diagnosed appropriately. However, a large portion of these women also specifically avoided getting diagnosed because they didn't want to be "labeled."

When I (and Katie) were in school in the 80s and 90s, mental health and treatment of kids labeled with particular "disorders," was...*not great.* It would vary school to school, but we did not have the tools nor the growing community of acceptance and support for mental diversity as we currently do. And, honestly, *even now*, the majority of parents I know with kids in schools still have a significant struggle to get their kids the support they need! "Retard," sadly, is still an insult to any kid who doesn't function—or can't pass—as someone with a "neurotypical" brain. (Workplaces, for my adult friends, also have a huge variance in acceptance and support for their neurodiverse employees.)

Furthermore, while we're discovering more of how mental functionality is a *spectrum*, we haven't the societal resources to adapt and support the fat ADHD girl who daydreams, gets high grades, but is told she's lazy and not trying hard enough because she can't manage long-term assignments...*and* the thin ADHD boy who can't sit still, forgets his homework, and is told he's a problem child and troublemaker that no one wants in class.

I embraced my ADHD diagnosis, and I believe an earlier diagnosis would have seriously helped with my health and

building my tools to thrive with how my brain works. But this isn't true for everyone. I currently help build support systems and communities for the neurodiverse folks out there because my freelance job and life allow me to. I have a great therapist and primary care doctor now, and I am not in a situation where I will face serious prejudice and persecution for openly claiming to be ADHD.

Because both Katie and Patti entrusted me, as a friend, with personal information regarding mental health, I don't want to share any specific points they disagree on regarding labels, mental health, or treatment. But I do want to speak about the decision parents face in getting their children diagnosed in regard to mental health. In line with Patti's (and Katie's, and my) philosophy, do your research and have open, honest conversation with your kids. There are *many more* resources available now than when Katie and I were young—hell, more than even ten years ago, when I was diagnosed. So as Patti and Peter included Katie and Christopher in the decisions about what schools they'd attend, include your kids in conversations about mental health. There are now books for all ages, as well as articles for parents and kids. (I've included some in the resources section.)

In much of my personal research upon getting diagnosed, I've found stories of people saying they intuitively knew, as early as six or seven, that they were different, and like me, they felt they would have benefited from that diagnosis' particular treatments. Some didn't receive those diagnoses due to the reasons I mentioned above—the complexity of interpreting symptoms, gender bias in research, or a lack of medical or psychological professionals in an area to accurately diagnose children. Others were not diagnosed because their parents chose not to without having open conversations with their children.

Mental health is a complex science. Our brains are *amazing*, and no two work exactly alike, so tools that work for one person, even if they have the same diagnosis (and that diagnosis is accurate), won't necessarily work for another. Also, many "flavors" of neurospicy have identical

symptoms—but different causes. As a very simplified metaphor, imagine you have a light flickering in your house. The bulb could be about to burn out. Or...the wiring is loose, a fuse needs to be replaced, something else is drawing power, an animal chewed on a wire leading to that light, water leaking from somewhere messed with that circuit, someone specifically wired that lamp to flicker... Each of these potential causes needs to be addressed differently.

And when it comes to "labeling," I am a fan of the term "neurospicy," and Patti was pretty tickled when I introduced her to it. It's inclusive and has (to me) a positive and empowering connotation. It also fit the metaphor of this book. If you've got a kid who's neurospicy, or you, yourself, are neurospicy—or both!—that will affect your recipe. Different people have different preferences for "spice," and there are so many different kinds of spice: curries, chilis, cinnamons, gingers, peppers, garlic, and other herbs and roots used by cooks from all parts of the world.

Using your intuition, employing your philosophy and beliefs, and guided by your unconditional love, a dash or heap of "neurospicy" can make your family meal uniquely delicious!

One version of Sabaluche's Famous Onion Pie that my family tried to recreate for the decades.

Chapter Eleven

A Recipe, Not a Box: Homework Snacks (Education Part 3)

*"Be impeccable with your word. Speak with integrity. Say only
what you mean. Avoid using the word to speak against yourself
or to gossip about others. Use the power of your word in the
direction of truth and love."*

– Don Miguel Rodriguez, *The Four Agreements*

Ensuring our children had a strong formal education—as
conventional or unconventional as that would be—was obviously a
priority for our family. But *school* is, in reality, only a small part of
what our children learn. Their greatest education comes from
watching their family, particularly their parents. Notice I said
"watching" their parents, not "listening to" their parents. The saying,
"They will do as we do, not as we say" is so freaking true!

For some of us, we learned things from our parents that were
things we *absolutely* disagree with and want to do differently. For me,
seeing my parents act incongruently from their words was one of
those things.

But to set the stage, let me take you back to a love story not very
different from mine and Peter's that led me to discover generations of

incongruence over...who was allowed to sit on the front porch (or "stoop," as we called it in New Jersey).

***

My parents grew up on the same street in Newark, New Jersey. Just a few houses apart! Believe it or not, they didn't meet or know each other even existed until they were both nineteen years old. Then, according to the stories told to my siblings and me, they ran into one another one fateful day, many miles away from their homes, down on the infamous "Jersey Shore" in Long Branch, NJ.

Dad's mother, Grandma Jenny, and their family were staying on the second floor of a rental home. Mom's mother, Grandma Lizzy (aka my "Sabaluche"), and their family were staying on the ground floor.

As my mom tells the story, it was just about love at first sight. "It was so strange. We were both emptying out the luggage and carrying it into the house. He looked a little familiar and was so handsome..."

This handsome man—my father!—offered to help her unpack. He shook my mother's hand and said, "Hi, I'm Armando, but everyone calls me Andy."

"Hi, I'm Ceal." As my mother, Ceal, introduced herself, Andy's mom had gotten out of the car—it was Jenny Giuliano from across the street! *What a small world!* Ceal thought, even as she noticed Andy's "big, strong hand," how polite and kind he'd acted, and how he'd helped her bring all the groceries and luggage inside. She'd liked him right away.

But as Andy came inside, helping Ceal with the luggage and groceries, Ceal's mom, my Sabaluche, stared him down and demanded, "Who-a you-a?"

Andy didn't even flinch. He went right over and introduced himself. "Hello, Mrs. Carola, I'm Armando Giuliano and live on Highland Avenue across the street from you. I brought my mom here for the summer, and I saw your daughter picking up all the heavy bags and wanted to offer my help. Are you okay if I continue to help?"

As they spoke, Ceal stood by the door, shaking in her shoes. Would her mother have a fit over this strange man coming into the house?

"That'sa nice, Armando," her mother said. "Tanka you for a helpa mya Celia."

Ceal was stunned!

According to my mom, after my dad helped his mom unpack, he came back and sat down with my grandmother. And to my mother's further shock, my grandmother said, "Celia, make-a the café fora Armando anda me." They sat and talked, and when he left, Sabaluche remarked, "He's-a nice-a boy. You like-a him?"

My mother didn't know what to say and just nodded her head. Barely a year and a half later, they were married!

***

It wasn't until my late teens—after I'd gone off to college—that I thought that much about my parents' first encounter. Now that I had my first boyfriend, I was curious about their love at first sight experience, and it struck me as odd that they'd lived almost right across the street from each other and hadn't met until they were nineteen. How did that happen?

During one of my college breaks, I finally asked my mom, "Why didn't you and dad know each other when you lived so close? Didn't you play together? Didn't you see each other at school? Didn't you see each other sitting on the stoop?"

My mother responded they'd gone to different schools—she public, my father Catholic—and she'd always played in the back yard. But then she said, "And I wasn't allowed to sit on the stoop. My mother forbade it."

That struck me as odd. "Why did Grandma forbid you from sitting on the stoop?"

"My mother said that only puttane—" Italian for whores. "—sit on the stoop. But your grandmother has her reasons..."

I was *very* interested in what those reasons could be since Sabaluche never forbade me from sitting on the stoop.

My mom explained, "The sister of the man your grandmother was going to marry in Italy, before she came to the United States, got pregnant out of wedlock, and the entire family was blackballed and shamed. So your grandmother's engagement was called off. No one was allowed to associate with that family. Everyone in the town spit on the sidewalk of the girl's parents' house every time they passed. That was the custom. And his sister used to sit on the stairs of her stoop, so your grandmother probably made the association in her mind that, because of that, all whores sat on the stoop. So of course, any young, beautiful woman who sits on the stoop must be looking for sex."

I was stunned at learning this new information.

But then my mother laughed. "Hmmm, I guess she thought I was so beautiful that all the men would want me if they saw me sitting there! And then I would get pregnant and shame her."

Holy shit! I very likely did *not* say that in front of my mom—though I'm sure I thought it. Instead, I said, "Grandma always let me sit on the stoop! Did she think I was a puttana? I've been sitting on that stoop for years... I had no idea. Thank God no one ever approached me asking for favors! What was the deal? Was Grandma trying to pimp me out?"

My mom laughed again. "Your grandmother was only strict with me. My brothers and my sister, Gerry, could do anything they wanted and were hardly ever punished. Your Aunt Gerry sat on the stoop all the time. Your grandmother would yell at her, and your Aunt Gerry would laugh and say back, 'If I am a puttana, then all the old ladies and men that are sitting on their stoops right now must also be puttane. And when you sit on the stoop, people must think you are a puttana too!' Then she ran before our mother could hit her with the wooden spoon."

After that conversation with my mother, I was not inclined to ask my grandmother for her side—especially because my mother also told me the rest of the sad story.

After being forbidden to marry the man she loved because his sister was a puttana, my twenty-three-year-old grandmother had secretly arranged to meet him before getting on the ship to the U.S. But her plans had been foiled because her parents had found out and taken her to another boat.

Side note: My grandmother, at the age of ninety-six, finally told me this story during a visit at my house. She cried, and I cried for her. "I-a loved-a him-a so mucha. I never loveda man-a like-a him again."

I could go on with all the questions I had about Grandpa, but this is not the time or place. (Maybe it'll go in another book someday...)

Sabaluche's perceptions were not always shared by everyone in the neighborhood. Or her children. She made a lot of assumptions (like the stoop), but I can see now that she had some deep wounds that affected her attitude about life, which probably lent to her tough persona. My mother wouldn't even *consider* speaking up to Sabaluche at any point in her life—up to the time Sabaluche passed.

I must have gotten that gene. I was afraid to talk back to my mom growing up—and then I went to college.

While in college, I discovered the women's liberation movement and began questioning *everything* that had a double standard. The idea that my grandmother thought all women sitting on the stoop were puttane bugged me every time I visited her. It took the newfound freedom I'd found after at least two years of college before I had enough bravery to confront her.

After dinner, while we were getting ready to watch wrestling on TV and Grandma was in a good mood, I finally asked, "Grandma, was my father allowed to sit on the stoop?

"Sí, sí, why-a not-a?"

"Well, why was the man allowed and not the women? Why didn't they call the men 'puttane?'"

Her response came with attitude. (Hmm... are you seeing a pattern in my family or what?) She said, in half English and half Italian (of course), "Whaddaya stupida? He's a mann-a non una donna."

"Oh really?" I responded with matching sass. Outrage made my voice higher and louder as I pressed, "So, you are telling me that *all* the women who sit on the stoop are putannes?"

"No, Iya not-a saya sucha ting!"

"Sure you did, Grandma. You never let my mom sit on the stoop!"

"You-a crazy, Poddi. Waddaya stupida? Me anda Rose Ferrone sitta ona the stoopa alla the time. We noa puttane."

It was pointless to argue. She'd either forgotten or been gaslighting me. In any case, I ended the conversation, and we sat down and cheered on Killer Kowalski.

With my newfound focus in college on societal inequalities, I started challenging the status quo of our Italian culture. It appeared to me that Italian men had complete freedom to do as they pleased. I never saw either one of my grandfathers lift a plate and put it in the sink after a meal. Nor did they ever say "thank you" to the cook. And if my brother were to start cleaning the dishes off the table, my grandmother would yell, "That'sa not a man'sa job. Your-a sistas, theya clean-a la tavola."

Our brother thought it was hilarious and would make faces at us behind Grandma's back, laughing that he was special. And he was! All Italian boys in my family, in my generation, were treated like gods—they could do no wrong and were to be waited on.

Furious at this injustice, I vowed that if I had a son, he would not get any preferential treatment. He would learn all the skills that a daughter would learn. He would not be pampered and grow up thinking that men had "men's" work and women had "women's" work. Whether son or daughter, my children would be treated equally.

When Peter and I met, we easily and organically worked in the office together as well as took care of the house together. He was very different from the men in my family. He helped clean the house and took care of the kids. Our kids witnessed parents that worked together and were cross-trained in all the duties of the family and household.

I remember my parents' amazed reaction when they visited and our children cleaned off the table and did the dishes without being told.

"Did you tell them they had to be on their best behavior because their grandparents are here?" my father asked.

"Actually no," I replied snarkily (clearly another family trait.) "That's their job. The cook doesn't do the dishes. We've always agreed as a family that we all contribute to the household. If Peter and I are paying the mortgage and buying the food, their jobs are to take away some of the household chores. We all help out in the ways we are capable of."

My dad just sat there with his mouth open a moment before stating, "We did that with you kids too."

I did not respond.

How would our children be treated equally? How would we teach our daughter and son they were equally capable and responsible as *people*? How would we help them grow into people who treated others equally, regardless of gender? *Justa you watcha me!* was our main mode of teaching. What they observed in us would be imprinted into their minds. And then, like every generation, they would do it differently than us when they moved into their own spaces and built their own families.

Between making sure our kids attended diverse schools and teaching them to reject unfairness and double standards, we set them up to be aware of societal changes in the world and to practice—and pass on—nonjudgemental acceptance of others' differences. And they have! Where I was motivated by the women's liberation movement to smash double standards and unfair treatment, starting with how I raised my children, the parents in my kids' generation are even further redefining expectations of gender and family.

In my forty-two years as a chiropractor taking care of many families, I've seen some of this progression. We've cared for two-mom families, two-dad families, non-gender-specific parents, and single parents (mostly moms save for one widower dad.)

The chiropractors (younger than our children!) who are now running our practice are especially conscientious and accepting of the different and nuanced pronoun usage by the newer patients coming into the office. I retired from practice right about the time that gender identity was exploding and expanded pronouns were being used more frequently, so I hadn't had a lot of exposure.

Until now.

I am currently involved in a higher education setting, and I am getting educated with a new vocabulary that better and more respectfully honors the identities of students, faculty, staff, and all their families. These newer generations of adults continue to break down older, more rigid, and less loving concepts, and they are raising a new generation that is even more tolerant, accepting, and expressing themselves more boldly.

I'm proud to see the work accomplished by our grown-up children living the values I'd wanted to instill in them as a parent. I applaud and respect them for their choices, and I'm learning from them new ways to follow my own intuition, dig deeper into my philosophy, and act in unconditional love.

***

Treating our kids as individual persons, regardless of gender was one thing. But what about little things many parents do where their actions don't line up with their words? Have you ever lied about your kids' ages in order to get a cheaper airfare, an all-you-can eat kid's meal at a restaurant, or entrance into a venue for less money?

If we were at one of my talks, I know I'd see a lot of nods—maybe some guilty faces—in the audience. I'm right there with you!

I mean, it's easy to justify that teensy bit of dishonesty, right? Our kid will be in our lap, they won't eat as much, we won't be in the park that long... There's a myriad of white lies we tell ourselves.

My parents held honesty in high value. Lying was *never* acceptable, or so we were taught. I remember one summer I was talking to a boy on vacation, but when my dad asked about it, I lied. Unfortunately, he knew otherwise. I talk more about this later, in my interlude on discipline, but for now, I'll tell you the punishment I received—particularly for *lying*—quite literally was pommeled into every fiber of my body.

Then on a later vacation to Disney, my parents lied about our ages to get cheaper admission tickets. I was really confused. And angry! How could it be alright for them to lie and capital punishment for me? I was old enough to know better, but young and scared enough not to confront them. This was way worse than me lying about talking to a boy!

What those actions taught me was that honesty was not, in fact, my parent's highest value. Saving money was. The whole incident left a huge impression on me, and it was another nail in the coffin of any trust I could put in my parents. If they'd explained their reasons to me, would that have justified things better in my mind? I can't say, except I still don't feel it was right—lying to save money, or even moreso, the double standard that I got a beating for my lie while they chose to lie, themselves. And, they were teaching me by example.

But let's jump forward in time several years. How would this experience affect how I'd raise my kids?

Our first plane trip with both kids happened in the early 90s, when kids under two could fly for free. Christopher was just over a year old, but Katie was turning three.

We reported Katie was under two years old when we got tickets. It saved a *lot* of money—and she *was* going to sit in my lap for the whole flight anyway, not in her own seat.

I remember the scene, sitting on that plane, so vividly.

As the flight attendant came down the aisle, my stomach cringed. I had a history of lying gone bad—and just remembering it was unpleasant.

She paused at our seats and asked, "Are both your kids under two years old?"

Both Peter and I looked up and lied through our teeth. "Yes. They are."

With a pleasant smile, she went on her way.

We'd gotten away with it!

My stomach, however, just got sicker. And sicker. Finally, I couldn't take it and quietly confessed to Peter, "I can't believe we lied. All I can think of is... I don't want to lie anymore!"

Peter understood. Later that night, we had a longer conversation and specifically decided to hold ourselves to the same standard as we wanted our kids to be held to. And we needed to start *now*, while they were little, so we were consistent by the time they became teenagers and could hold our incongruences against us. There should be no double standard when it came to values. Even though they were little and probably didn't pick up on what we'd done on the plane, we felt the discordant energy and never lied like that again.

In case you're wondering, no, Peter and I didn't go back and pay for Katie's ticket. We are still imperfect humans.

Speaking of being imperfect humans, there were plenty of other situations where we weren't as careful or self-aware as we wanted to be. Maybe you can relate.

Has your kid ever asked you when you were going to do something and you said, "just a couple of minutes?"

And then, before you know it, *ten* minutes have passed?

Well, Katie, who has always taken things quite literally, was and is very good about calling me out when I've made such a mistake. Just as clearly as that plane ticket incident, I can remember a few times where I'd say we'd go to the playground or do some task or play some game in "a couple of minutes." And, inevitably, I'd get distracted, and like a clock, at about the ten-minute mark, Katie would let me know with a full tantrum.

"You said a couple of minutes, Mommy, and it's been *way* more than that!"

Holy shit! I *really* needed honor my word or my kids would lose their trust in me!

So, when called out on "breaking my word" and losing track of time, I would apologize. "Katie, I am so sorry. Mommy lost track of time, and I will come right now. See, I am putting down all the dishes, and I will do them later. Let's go."

And then there were the times I would ask Christopher to do a chore for me, and he would say, "Sure, Mom. I can do that in a few minutes."

An hour later, because I, too, had lost track of time, I would ask him if he finished.

"I'm sorry, Mom. I got distracted. I'll do it right now."

I was infuriated, but then I'd realize he'd had a good teacher. *Shit!* I hate when my actions come full circle and bite me in the ass!

As difficult as it was in the moment, this practice of acknowledging and apologizing worked out in the long run. Just recently, my thirty-something-year-old daughter came to visit Peter and me in San Francisco. We were getting ready to go out for dinner, and Katie asked me, "How long until we leave the room, Mom?"

I jokingly said, "In a few minutes. Which is probably more like ten minutes, just like I would say to you when you were little. Do you remember accusing me of lying?"

"Yes, Mom!" she answered with a smirk on her face.

We both had a good laugh over that.

***

It is so hard to break the mold from the boxes we grew up in. My parents' generation had it harder than mine. Why do I think that? Because their parents *demanded* respect, but didn't often reciprocate that respect, and the punishment was much harsher if you didn't obey their (many) rules.

Remember the stoop story? I fully believe my mom, consciously or unconsciously, did not want to parent us the way she'd been parented. And I followed suit, determining what values I wanted to instill in my children and listening to my inner voice as to what the best way to love them would be. My mom did it her way, and I have come to respect that and be more compassionate towards her. After all, she had Sabaluche for a mom!

Something to remember, though, is that people may not realize when they're acting incongruently to what they believe. Especially if "do as I say, not as I do," was part of their upbringing—and if those who *taught* that lesson also didn't realize their contradictory lessons.

I'd been allowed to sit on the stoop by my grandmother and my mother. Neither gave me a good explanation of why they didn't hold me to the same rules and expectations my mother had been held to. In retrospect, I can guess they were slowly changing their belief system —that what they believed was shifting from what they'd been raised to believe.

And, as I learned sitting on that plane and lying about Katie's age, it can be truly uncomfortable and painful to realize that your actions are not aligning with your beliefs. Sometimes we can lean into that discomfort the way we lean into the discomfort of adding a new exercise routine or dietary change into our lives. Other times, we can't. At least not easily.

Through my adult years, I would take my grandmother, Sabaluche, shopping. After that, she typically wanted to go to the diner for lunch. After the meal, she would pick up a fork (or a spoon or a salt shaker) and say, "I'ma missa the forka justa like-a this one. Poddi, putta inna you pock."

Horrified—especially after my parents' "lessons" in honesty, since stealing fit in the same category as lying, particularly in respect to the punishment it invoked—I would whisper back, "Grandma, that is stealing! I could get in trouble."

"Fongul, you sunnamuhbeech. Putta inna you pock!" she would say more sternly, wrapping whatever object she'd claimed in a napkin and trying to shove it into my hand or pocketbook if she could. "They-a have-a lotta money more-a than-a me. They-a won'ta missa this. Now putta inna you pock!"

I was taught to know better! But I'd also been taught to do whatever my parents or grandparents (or aunts and uncles even) told me to do. And if I disobeyed or disrespected an elder family member I was punished worse. What could I do?

All-Grown-Up Patti complied and putta the forka inna her pock as demanded. I told my mother about it, and she just said, "Welcome to the club. I've been doing that for years!"

Holy shit! See why I came to respect and be more compassionate to my mom?

When Sabaluche passed away, my mom gave me a few of her things, one of them her beautiful, carved, wooden silverware box. She handed me the box with an eager look—possibly a smirk. (Family trait, like I said.)

Well, I kinda had an idea it wasn't going to be thousands of dollars' worth of fine silver. I opened it, ready for anything. Inside: Every fork, spoon, knife—none matching!—from every Grand Theft Flatware escapade where she'd made me or one of my siblings (or my mom!) an accomplice.

I've told that story hundreds of times, and while it's usually followed by laughter, angst still balls up in the pit of my stomach—just like after I opened that silverware box. Those "adventures" could have gone very bad, very quickly.

But that was part of the box I grew up in: Stealing (or lying) was "okay" if it could be justified by someone who had more power than me—even though I knew, in my gut, it was wrong. (Which also led to questioning my intuition when it pulled me away from that box of rules I knew.)

So if you're trying to break out of patterns you learned and don't agree with, if you find yourself struggling to follow the same standards you want your kids to live up to, I feel you. If you're a hugger, let me give you a big one! It's freaking hard!

You're going to fail sometimes. Maybe a *lot* of times. It's okay. Own it—as painful as that can be—and continue working to do better.

And if your kids call you out? That's also not exactly fun, but think of it this way: They're learning the *real* lesson you want them to, right? If they see you make mistakes, take responsibility for your actions, and still keep trying, and then you're *living* the education you want for them.

I've said it multiple times in this book, and *countless* times in life, my children are my greatest teachers—particularly Katie who still doesn't hesitate in calling out her seventy-year-old mother whenever she's not acting in congruence with what she's saying. You know what, though? She definitely learned *that* from me too!

When Katie was two weeks old, I got a very distressed telephone call from my parents. My mom and dad were sharing the receiver of their landline (this was pre-cell phone ages), and both of them blurted out some form of "Did you know your sister was dating a black man for the past twenty years?"

Uh... Duh! The rest of us siblings *knew*—just as we *knew* not to specifically mention that to our parents. Innocently, I asked, "You didn't know?"

"No!" Both of them rapid-fired responses at me, and I couldn't follow who was saying what. "How would we know? We thought they were just friends. And now she wants to bring him to the house for dinner! We can't allow that! If she stays with him, she will not be allowed in the house again."

When they stopped talking, I let the dead air stretch. I couldn't believe my ears. Were they joking?

Growing up, our parents had taught us to accept everyone, no matter the color of their skin. My father had made it a point to tell us about the non-Italian, non-Caucasian people he'd hired in the store he managed. "They're good workers! They are well-behaved! They dress nicely!" He was proud of himself and his non-discriminatory nature.

Linda was living true to what he'd boasted about.

After I let the silence hang, I pulled myself together and asked, "Why do you have a problem with Ed being black? Didn't you teach us not to discriminate?"

My dad answered, "He may be a very nice man, but not for our family. What would our friends and relatives think?" (Most of my aunts and uncles made disparaging comments about blacks and other races, so they would not be very open to Linda dating a black man.) "And what if they have babies? Their kids will be ridiculed and teased by the other kids in school."

I wanted to laugh at that one! Little did he know that my sister had no intention of having kids, but that was another conversation, so I just said, "I think any possible kids will be alright, but what about Linda? She's your daughter, right? You love and accept her one day and want to disown her the next because she is with a black man?"

My father kept sputtering on how it wasn't right and he wouldn't stand for it! "She needs to leave him!"

Nothing I said was getting through. I looked down at the baby in my arms, the newborn granddaughter my father would doubtlessly cherish, and something erupted deep inside me. How *dare* they! All the years of their double standards, lies, scoldings, and beatings... Of feeling weak and vulnerable to their whims all came swirling out like a giant tornado. I needed to protect my sister and have them wake up to what they were saying.

I was a thirty-four-year-old mom, and I'd *never* spoken back to my father. As if I were possessed, calm and determined words just left my mouth: "If you don't accept Edward, you will never see your granddaughter again." And I hung up.

My intuition had taken over. And I'd meant what I said. At the time, I honestly had no idea how he would react. What had I done to my family dynamic? To my new daughter's and my future relationship with my parents?

Two days later, my parents called back. My dad said, "Well, we thought about what you said. We'll have Linda and Edward over and have a conversation."

***

Having the experiences I'd had with my family and knowing my children would be in the hands and values of the teachers at whatever schools they attended created a lot of angst for me. I wanted our children to be in a safe space, so to speak, exposed to teachers that shared our values, teachers that encouraged critical thinking, and teachers that would not impose or force their perspectives on our children. Miraculously, we found schools that fit those requirements.

But we also knew how much of our kids' education would come directly from us.

Even if we hadn't been as lucky or blessed as we were in their schooling journey, we needed to be teachers they could trust for all their life. And we couldn't just stand up and *tell* them what to do; we needed to live the lessons we were imparting.

And the core of those lessons?

You guessed it—exactly what I'm sharing with you in this book.

Listen and trust your intuition.

Have a clear philosophy and set of beliefs to guide your actions.

Choose to love unconditionally.

It's a great recipe to tuck into any lunch—for you and your kids!

*Initials and abbreviations used to respect the privacy of certain friends.

Coffee Break

Recipe for Discipline.
Leave the Old; Create the New

*"It is easier to build strong children
than to repair broken men."*

- Frederick Douglass

After my children were born, I was hesitant to let my parents watch them without me or Peter around. And when I finally got the courage to do so, I was shaking as I told them they were not to *ever* put a hand on them—not even a pat on the bum—no matter what!

To my utter shock, my dad replied, "Your mother and I never laid a hand on any of you kids, so why would we do that with your kids?"

My mother attested to his veracity!

My jaw dropped. *WTF?!* That was not the childhood I remembered.

***

To anyone outside our family, my father was nothing but a great guy: a dedicated husband and good father. He worked ninety hours a week (literally), provided for his family, and would give you the shirt off his back.

This is what I knew growing up:

I was the goody-goody of my siblings, but one time I dared retrieve some cutoff jeans and moccasins from the trash, where my father had thrown them. A few weeks later, a neighbor caught me wearing them and told my dad. He beat me until I pissed my pants—and I'm not exaggerating.

When I was fifteen and we were on vacation, I lied about talking to a boy. I don't remember how he knew I'd lied, but I remember being hit until I pissed again. On top of being grounded for the entirety of our vacation. Bad enough I talked to some boy I shouldn't have talked to (according to some stupid rule), but the *big* reason for my capital punishment was lying to my parents.

One morning, my father drove to the bus stop to see if my brother had the ear flaps of his hat pulled down. He didn't. Dad brought him home and beat the living shit out of him, whacking his head against the door jamb and giving him a bloody nose.

Mom did nothing to stop this. Neither did I. I'm still horrified telling this story.

And then there was the time my fourteen-year-old sister came home after curfew from a date with her seventeen-year-old boyfriend. I was in the bedroom I shared with my sisters when I heard her run up the stairs, followed by my dad's heavier footsteps. They burst into the room, and my dad started yelling. I shook under my covers, knowing what would happen. But she yelled right back at him! I'd never done that. And when he raised his hand to her, she raised hers right back and screamed, "If you fucking hit me, I'll fucking hit you right back!"

Time stopped. My father turned around and walked down the stairs.

Why hadn't I ever thought to do that? I remember thinking to myself.

After *that* night, it was true—to my knowledge—that he and Mom never raised a hand to any of us again.

***

Let's fast forward past that first time I would leave my children alone with my parents.

I forgave them.

I mean it, honest-to-God, I really forgave them. But it took a lot of time, therapy, and self-work.

I attended a week-long personal growth retreat called the Hoffman Quadrinity Process[10], where I had the realization that my parents were "guilty, but not to blame" for who they were as parents and how that landed on me and my siblings. This particular *holy shit* epiphany freed me from the emotional baggage I was carrying against my parents that kept me from trusting either of them or wanting to grow our relationship. For the first time, I could honestly tell them, "I love you."

But why forgive them?

Because they didn't know better. All they knew was how they were brought up. My dad had an alcoholic father who'd come home drunk every night. I have no idea if he'd ever beaten my dad, but I suspect so, and that's where he learned the behavior. Even in his later years, my father never held a grudge and spoke lovingly about his father.

I also want to point out that, among my family, in our neighborhood, in this time (50s-60s), the stories I shared above were the norm. Besides what my father did, I recall my mother calling my uncle from upstairs to sit next to me with a belt until I finished my peas. My parents' actions were supported by their peers, other parents with similar draconian discipline practices.

Even before I had this epiphany of forgiveness, I'd seen my father change when he met his first grandchild, my daughter, Katie.

My dad was a kind, loving grandpa who was sensitive to Katie's uniqueness. When they would come to visit, he knew not to expect Katie to come running to greet him. He'd learned to wait for her to approach him—or face her wrath.

He even boasted to me, "I have her figured out. I wait until she is ready for me to approach her, and I do it very cautiously."

I was proud of his sensitivity to her and *pissed* he'd never been like that with me!

But Katie had treated him how I wished I'd treated him. She made boundaries and communicated them. He listened.

But Peter and I had also *taught* Katie how she should expect people to treat her.

I'd never thought to do that because I'd grown up in a strict household that enforced children only speak when spoken to, they do not question their parents, and they would suffer consequences for stepping outside the boundaries others set *for* them.

I vowed I would never do that to my kids. I would be different. I would communicate with them in an understanding way, and I would *never* stand by, as my mother did, if I saw my child being abused.

Since I followed my heart and intuition and married Peter, who shared the same values I held, I kept that vow. And while I'd be lying if I said I *always* communicated in an understanding way, I definitely had a different discipline strategy than my parents did.

Kids need boundaries, and Peter and I wanted to create them in a way that would teach our children how to develop their own. That meant we needed to model the behaviors we wanted; we couldn't be hypocritical and demand "do as I say, not as I do." If we wanted our children to value non-violent solutions, we couldn't act in violence. Our repertoire of discipline included clear communication and sincere apologies; time outs; restricted access to games, computers, television, time with friends; extra chores and responsibilities; and making sure the punishment was equitable to the infraction. It didn't include corporal punishment.

Of course, just a few months ago Katie asked me, "Mom, do you remember the time you hit me on my head with the dishtowel?"

That was a moment of frustration that we probably all have had as parents. But it wasn't a *beating.* Knowing how deliberately Peter and I chose our disciplinary actions, I was confident I could joke back, "You're lucky it wasn't something of more substance!"

We both laughed.

I want to take a moment and acknowledge that some of you reading this may have had—or still have—abusive parents with whom it's *not* safe to let them back into your life or your children's lives. First of all, I give you so much love and respect for where you are right now and the work you're doing for yourself and your children. If you were here and open to it, I'd give you the biggest hug! Forgiveness, in and of itself, is not an act for whom you forgive, but a gift and tool for your own healing. I'm not here to tell you what to do; I'm sharing what's worked for me. Secondly, and I'll repeat this over and over because it's the truth: adjust your parenting recipe for what *you* and *your family* needs. Do I believe in the recipe I'm teaching? Absolutely. Just as strongly, I believe you should personalize the hell out of it!

Our philosophy led us to make clear what boundaries we'd instill in our children and what type of discipline we'd teach them if they crossed those boundaries. Intuition helped us realize when one of our children was deliberately disrespecting boundaries, didn't realize what they were doing, or if their behaviors were something else altogether—thus informing what level of discipline we needed. And our unconditional love reminded us that all our actions, even discipline, were because we truly wanted the best for these souls we'd been given to raise.

Just as my gluten-free, sage and butter Gavadeel is drastically changed from what my grandmother prepared, our discipline style shares the same tenets I believe my parents held—to raise happy, good, and successful children—but is an entirely different flavor than what I was served as a child.

You need to find the right "flavor" and nutritional needs for your family regarding your children's discipline. And guess what? Your children will also find their own flavor for disciplining their kids—which will probably be different from yours.

Let's make a toast to doing our best as parents with the ingredients we have—even for the difficult stuff.

Salut!

Chapter Twelve

The Chef's Work: Perfect Patti's Transformation

*"As I've always said, cooking is a philosophy; it's not a recipe [...]
so therefore, it's not just teaching them how to cook, it's sharing
your philosophy and your vision with them. It's as simple as
that."*

– Marco Pierre White

My sisters and I have been trying to perfect our Sabaluche's onion pie for decades. We even enlisted our cousins, Rosi and Vincent, on the quest, as well as my son Christopher, for his baking and engineering perspective that started with our Nieman Marcus chocolate chip cookies. Every year, when we get together to hopefully get it right once and for all, we fail again. We are all using the same type of flour, tomatoes, olive oil, onions and cheese! WTF?

Was there a secret ingredient that Sabaluche used that we missed? Why didn't we write down the recipe?

I never asked Sabaluche; I didn't want a repeat of when I asked her for the Gavadeel recipe. I wasn't ready to be questioned if I was "a-stupida" yet again.

With every failed attempt, we get even more frustrated that we are unable to reproduce Grandma's unquestionably amazing onion pie. Like a unicorn, it only appeared on rare, unexpected occasions—

only when Sabaluche felt like making it!

Mention onion pie to any of my family or friends who had been there when that fabled treat was coming out of the oven, and the orgasmic look on their face tells it all. And they all say, "Oh my God! Sabaluche made the best onion pie. I don't know anyone else that has ever made something that delicious. I wish I had some now."

So what's the secret to perfecting the recipe?

Not just Sabaluche's onion pie recipe, but your parenting recipe…

Come closer, I'm going to tell you.

Even closer. It's a secret. I've sprinkled it through this whole book and hoped you'd find it.

Lean just a little closer. I'll whisper it to you…

It was something that Sabaluche possessed. Along with every grandma in the world who cooks with an intensity and passion for her kids and her grandkids. It's in every famous chef and every cook who takes pride in their specialty.

And, as I came to find out, it was in me. It's also in *you* and every parent striving to perfectly nourish their children.

It is something special that comes *from you* as you become the person and parent that you are.

We cannot quantify it, we cannot measure it, but we know it is there.

What *is* that secret ingredient?

IT'S THE CHEF!

It's you and me!

What I came to recognize in the process of writing this book is that I always, as a mother, strove to honor the recipe: to trust my intuition, keep true to my values, and above all, act from my heart.

Sabaluche followed that recipe! She never faltered. She loved us through the food she prepared. That was her love language—without condition.

And before you pushed away from the table, she expected to hear it was the best food you had ever tasted! (Sound familiar?)

Here's the thing though: My family still hasn't been able to recreate Sabaluche's onion pie.

That's not the point. It's not about making "Sabaluche's Onion Pie." It's about creating and *following* that same recipe of *nourishing the ones you love in a way only you can do.*

I didn't get that for a long time.

Just like I thought there was only one *best* onion pie—my grandmother's—I also thought in order to be the Best Mom on the Planet, I had to be Perfect Patti.

Who is Perfect Patti? Let me introduce you...

***

Once upon a time, there was a little girl from New Jersey who was the best-behaved little girl out of four siblings. (Okay, I'm not sure if my siblings would agree.) She was smart, went to Catholic school, and even went to school to be a doctor—what every parent wants for their kid, right? Then she married her perfect partner. His name even started with the same letter, perfect for those monogrammed wedding and anniversary presents!

Perfect Patti was going to be that mom who was relentlessly calm, a font of wisdom, and an endless source of organic, home-made healthy food for her kids—and all their friends. And they would all wish their moms were just like her. She was going to have a perfect house, perfect children, and a perfect relationship, all while maintaining a career that required utmost perfection.

Perfect Patti and her perfect husband would walk through grocery stores and see those kids in carts screaming for M&Ms at exhausted-looking parents and secretly share smug smiles because *they* would never be *those* parents and *their children* would never be like *those* kids.

This was actually a fantasy I'd fully convinced myself would be the truth.

Before I had kids, of course.

Hilarious, I know! Our delusional fantasies shattered once we actually became parents. We didn't listen (at least I know I didn't) when our friends with living, breathing, unruly, screaming, and having-tantrums-in-the-grocery-store kids, promised us, "Wait until you have your own kids—it's intense!"

Want to guess how things went when we did have our own kids?

Go ahead and laugh. Fortunately, now I'm in a place where I can laugh right along with you.

***

My relationship with Perfect Patti has been and still is complicated.

I *was* the goody-goody of my family. If you read the last coffee break, you heard about the few *worst* things I'd gotten punished for: I had the audacity to wear ripped jeans and moccasins (utterly scandalous!). And then I *dared* sneak such disreputable clothing items from the trash and *wear them again!* Lastly, I dared talk to a boy—and then *lie* about it.

The devil totally has a special pitchfork set aside for me based on that, I'm sure.

On top of my model behavior, I was a smart kid. I *am* a smart woman! My parents did brag about my reading abilities at a young age, just like they proudly recounted to relatives and friends about a whole play I'd put together for Christmas dinner entertainment. I was sent to Catholic school, and though it felt like a prison, I was an *excellent* student. I graduated high school with honors, and I got my doctorate in chiropractic (*magna cum laude*) when only ten percent of our class were women!

I *could* pull off being Perfect Patti with some regularity. Or at least do a fantastic job of *looking* like I was pulling it off. I had "fake it 'til ya' make it" down to a science. Down to a point where even I would have a hard time telling when I was "faking" it.

But Patti, you might be thinking, *isn't that the goal? Fake it 'til you're successful and no longer faking it?*

Let me give you two *bonus* secrets:

1. You can successfully fake yourself into forgetting who your *authentic* self is. *That* should not be the goal. You could be a wonderfully successful person and still not be your *best self*. Your *best self* is your authentic *self*—living true to who you are in your most fulfilling life.

2. It is IMPOSSIBLE to be perfect all the time.

Through my life, into parenthood, I was trying to be Perfect Patti. *All* the time. What my kids—my whole family—wanted and needed was for me to be *me*.

Let me tell you, trying to be Perfect Patti was exhausting and detrimental to my health. I could list hundreds of stories where I tried to be Perfect Patti and ended up feeling wounded and victimized. Hell, that's one of the reasons I wrote this book! I felt like many moms around me were having the "perfect" parenting experience, their lives just rainbows and blue skies. What was wrong with me? Why wasn't anyone talking about the challenges and the craziness and the amount of time and energy parenting required? Or all the angst those little buggers caused us?

As I look back, some parents did give honest accounts. Others? Maybe they were ashamed or afraid to reveal their vulnerabilities. Or maybe they were faking it 'til they made it.

But Perfect Patti was in her own delusional world and blaming herself.

"It must be me," I said to myself over and over. "Something's wrong with me."

So here we are: My kids are grown-ups in their thirties, married and living on their own. I have written this book and shared my parenting stories hoping others may find some solace in seeing someone else who was not always the perfect parent.

Not only was I not always perfect, I made it harder on myself (and my family) in my mission to be Perfect Patti! I didn't want to let myself—or anyone else—down. And God forbid I showed signs that I was challenged to my deepest core.

As a parent, and as a person, Patti—the *authentic* Patti—had a lot to learn.

***

I love the mother-son lunches I have with Christopher! Not only do I learn how he's doing and what's going on in his life, but he also still gives me lessons I need for myself.

On one particular lunch, I remember asking him if he was happy with his job and if he had any thoughts of looking for something better with more pay.

He said that a position had opened up where he worked that was an advancement, but it would require some more training on his part and not be exactly what he loved to do. Then he added, "But I'm very happy doing what I'm doing. I'm not really interested in a new position or looking elsewhere, even if I could make more money."

I told him I supported whatever decision he made and the most important thing was that he was happy, but when I was driving home, I panicked. Was it my fault he wouldn't progress in his career or life? Had I failed to motivate him to always strive for more?

Let me back up and tell you why I was thinking that.

You see, in grammar school, Christopher won award after award for excellence in math and computers. Then, one day, he came to me having a meltdown—very unlike my son!

In between sobs, he confessed, "I don't think I can keep up with all this work my teachers are giving me!" He'd been told by the school that he could get the highest mathematics recognition of anyone who'd attended the school if he just pushed harder and did more work in the next few months before graduation. "But I don't care about that. It's just too much for me, and I don't know what to do about it."

My son was miserable and stressed out like I'd never seen him before.

My response needed to honor him, but at the same time, it should be a learning moment. I was conflicted:

Do I push him? Tell him life will present him with challenges like this and he would get stronger if he just pushed through?

Or do I trust my gut and stay true to my values—values I had instilled in my children?

I was a self-proclaimed MAH (Mother Against Homework). Peter and I believed kids should come home from a long day of school and go outside and play. School had its place, but kids needed to be outside, exploring, playing, and creating in an open environment without someone standing over them.

I also knew there was another agenda at work. A few weeks prior, one of Christopher's teachers had pulled me aside to tell me about this fantastic opportunity for my son: the highest academic achievement in mathematics in the school's history. How awesome would that be for his resume? (And what great PR for the school!)

But a voice inside me was crying. Was I really willing to put my son through hell for that? It would be against our values. On top of that, Christopher did *not* like to be in the spotlight; he was an introvert.

(I'm still grappling with the fact that a child of mine could actually be an introvert!)

All of these thoughts erupted in my mind in a split second, but it felt like forever.

I sat my son down in front of me, looked into his distraught face, and listened to my heart and gut. "Christopher, I know that you are working your butt off and now you are being pushed to go above and beyond what you want to do for the recognition of being the best in mathematics. Is this something that is important to you? Your grades and effort at school are already beyond commendable. Your dad and I are so proud of you, and I feel like *you* should get to choose how much further you want to go. We will support your decision, no matter what."

It was like a switch was flipped. He lit up with relief and joy. Hugging me, he said, "I love you, Mom," and then went outside and kicked around the soccer ball.

Christopher didn't bring the topic up again. I, however, spent God knows how long second-guessing myself. Did I choose the right words? Would it have a negative effect on him?

When graduation day finally rolled around, imagine my surprise when the headmistress announced, "We are proud to award Christopher Kevorkian the highest achievement in mathematics in the *history* of Delphi Academy!"

That rascal! How many nights of sleep had I lost worrying if I'd given him the best advice? Worrying if I should have pushed him, not given him an "out"!

Weeks after the mother-son lunch where Christopher had told me he wasn't looking for a better position or higher pay, I was chatting with a friend and digging up all those same worries, thoughts, and fears. The Perfect Patti who still lives in my head "rent free" (as I think the kids are saying now?) was having a fit. Had my choice to not push him as a kid stalled his career, set him up to not be as successful as he could be?

My friend asked me, "Is he happy?"

"As far as I know, yes. Very happy."

"So, he's doing what he loves. He and his wife are making enough money for all they need and all the things they want to do, right?"

"As far as I know, yeah..." What she was getting at was beginning to dawn on me.

"Then you've just proven you've done a great job parenting because you raised a kid who's found balance! At thirty-something! Isn't that the whole goal of life? He's *happy* and fulfilled. Why should he feel he ought to change that?"

Holy shit!

My advice to Christopher twenty-plus years ago came from the deepest part of me that valued teaching our children to have balance in their lives. I didn't realize it at the time, but he was forming his values. I had intuitively sensed it and gave him the best advice I could have in that scenario. Phew!

It was definitely something the thirty-something-year-old Patti *hadn't* achieved—though she did her damnedest to make it look like she had.

If you were on the outside, watching me try to be Perfect Patti with two young children, you might think I was doing great! The truth was, I was struggling. Sometimes I was struggling so hard I was *literally* making myself sick.

Like after Christopher was born and I'd thought I'd had a stroke.

The woman living her dream of being a chiropractor, a holistic doctor, was unknowingly *harming her own body* by trying to be Superwoman: nursing two kids and pushing herself to be and do everything for everyone in her family to her own detriment. Trying to be someone she wasn't to please everyone was making her sick.

Funny how the universe will hit us with a two by four to get us to listen sometimes.

It would be over a decade later for me to be the mother who would tell Christopher—when he was on the brink of making himself sick with stress—how proud she was of all his hard work, how he had to evaluate what he wanted most, and how he'd be supported, no matter what he chose. But imagine, *imagine*, if I could've been that mom to myself earlier! "I'm proud of my hard work! What is right for me? I have the support I need, no matter what."

And just in case *you* need it, *you*, picking up this book and probably piles of others, watching parenting videos, working hard to educate yourself to be the best parent—best person—you can be. I'm proud of you! What does your gut say is the right thing for you? Listen to that voice. I support your loving effort, however it looks for you and *your* family.

How often do any of us find ourselves unable to do what we know is right—right for ourselves, our family, our world—because it will make too many waves? Because we're spoiling the *appearance* of things being "right"? What do you think living with that internal incongruence can do to a person?

For me, it bred a lot of resentment growing up. Remember my story about those ripped jeans and moccasins that my dad threw out and I liberated from the trash? That was me trying to express another aspect of who I was, of how I wanted people to see me. Both the first time I wore those clothes and when I was caught wearing them again, I was *beaten* as punishment. Just for choosing to wear clothing *someone else* deemed to be inappropriate for me. And I resented my parents for years because of it!

Fortunately, I did leave home and go to college, where I was able to delve into the world of self-discovery. In college, people were experimenting with psychedelics (it *was* the 60s!) to open their minds and access more of themselves. I discovered sources like Richard Alpert (Ram Dass) and his book, *Be Here Now*[11]. That book, which I still have in my library today, was an important influence in my personal growth. Richard and his colleague, Timothy Leary, were raising their consciousness at Harvard and learning first-hand about self-discovery using LSD[12]. (I chose not to take that path! As I am known to say, "There are many ways to Nirvana.")

As I delved more deeply into my own consciousness during my college years, I felt empowered to express myself more. I could be openly smart and capable, supported by the friends that I surrounded myself with. That, coupled with the emerging women's liberation movement, helped with my self-esteem and how I showed up in my life.

The *real* Patti was beginning to blossom.

Yet even with all the personal growth and enlightenment I was experiencing, I still worried about what people thought of me. I was still on that Perfect Patti quest.

***

My life made a major shift when I went to chiropractic school. I loved learning about the body. And I'd found my people—people who shared my values in health and wanted to change the world for the better. I was empowered with the knowledge I was acquiring and the confidence growing deep inside me. After graduating in October of 1982, I moved to Boston and opened my practice a few months later. I was prepared, passionate, motivated, and certain that I would be successful.

My parents were excited for me and wanted me to succeed. So much so that my mother felt the need to offer me unsolicited advice when I opened my practice: "Patricia, now that you are a doctor, you need to dress like a doctor. You can't wear your sweats and tee shirts to the office."

To which I replied, quite snarkily, "You know, Mom, now that I'm a doctor, whatever I wear is what a doctor would wear!"

Holy Shit!

First, I could never have stood up to my mother even a few months prior. Something was happening to me. My Jersey was emerging. It felt so good to stand up to my mom and not be afraid of her saying, "Wait until your father comes home!"

But secondly, there she was, telling me once again what to wear— what was "appropriate" in her critical eyes. I wish I'd said that I still had the moccasins and cutoffs, and *that* was going to be my "doctor" outfit!

Even with my newfound sassiness, as I grew my practice, a part of me held to the belief that I needed to be someone I wasn't. I still held back from expressing the full greatness and brilliance that I knew was inside of me.

And then, about eight years into my practice, an angel appeared in the form of a very wise patient who handed me a piece of paper with words from Marianne Williamson:

> Our greatest fear is not that we are inadequate. Our deepest fear is that we are powerful beyond measure. It is our light, not our darkness that most frightens us. We ask ourselves "who am I to be brilliant, gorgeous, talented, fabulous?" Actually, who are you not to be? Your playing small does not serve the world. We are born to make manifest the glory of God that is within us. And as we let our own light shine, we unconsciously give other people permission to do the same.

HOLY SHIT!

Holy Shit right to my core!

By playing small and not letting myself "shine," I was keeping other people from realizing *they* could shine to *their* fullest. Why was I doing that to myself? Is that something I would have wanted to model for my children?

I think about this *Holy Shit* moment on a regular basis, especially as a parent. I want my kids to see me shine so they will shine. I want them to be empowered to know that they are brilliant beyond measure and that by shining their light, they give others permission to do the same.

Learning to let yourself shine—*authentically* shine—is hard work though. It's easier to put the time and effort into empowering your kids to be authentic and shine.

We were blessed to be able to be selective about their schools: What were their values and what example was being emulated by their teachers? Did the school allow their teachers to trample and ridicule their students? My third-grade teacher did that to me. She called me up to the front of the room and lowered my grade for self-control because I yelled out an answer when she didn't call on me. That embarrassment convinced me to dull my shine for a very long time.

Would the school encourage my children to express their individuality? Particularly after my cut-offs and moccasins event, I didn't restrict my kids from wearing clothes they liked or even getting piercings or tattoos. (One of them did; the other didn't.)

We encouraged our children to share their ideas. They weren't punished for having a different opinion from their parents.

But here's the thing: While my husband and I consciously chose to not inhibit or discourage our children's enthusiasm and self-expression, I was still policing my own.

Perfect Patti *could* shine. As I said, I was smart, capable, and *fantastic* at making it look like everything was shiny and perfect. But Perfect Patti was conceived, gestated, and born from the praise and punishment she received based on *other people's* expectations. In trying to be—in thinking I *had* to be—Perfect Patti, I was not being, not *shining*, my perfect *self*.

I was trying to be the perfect representation of empowerment—of the Perfect Patti perception of empowerment—that I wanted my kids to aspire to. And it was exhausting! I was not expressing my truest self, and as I look back, that kind of compromise was not the best attribute to teach my kids.

I was creating discordance in myself: encouraging my children to be authentic while not practicing what I preached. My true self felt it, and so did my kids.

Even after going through significant self-work through my life, experiencing major breakthroughs, I recall a time when my daughter was *in her twenties* and we were having another of our—let's call it *animated*—conversations. I hit a breaking point. I'd felt like I'd been walking on eggshells around her for too long, not wanting to hurt her feelings or ignite her temper (that she *totally* didn't get from me), and I utterly and thoroughly lost it at her. I swore at her up, down, sideways, and every which way. Every moment I'd held back, every time I wanted to spew what was *really* on my mind just came gushing out.

And when I was done?

My daughter smiled at me. "Mom I am so glad that you finally let your Jersey out! I have been waiting for you to do that for a long time. I am so proud of you!"

Holy shit! Why did I wait so long to express my true feelings? And by waiting so long, it came out like an earthquake—but it felt so good!

And how did my little girl get to be so freakin' smart?

***

If you ask most parents when their job is done, they'll tell you it's never done. Even when their kids are off in the world with their own lives, their own partners (if they want partners), and their own kids (if they want kids), your vocation as a parent is still there. (And I'll get to *that* in the next couple of chapters, I promise.)

That means your job to make yourself the best person you can be is also never finished. Life reveals things that might shift your perspective, your body will change with age and environment, and you'll face challenges that will alter how you experience life in little ways—or in very big ways. You *always* have something more to learn about yourself.

Or your long-time quest to perfect a family recipe.

My editor, Trish, has been a family friend for about twenty-five years or so. On her first visit to our practice, Katie recognized her as a kindred spirit and adopted her on the spot. Even after Trish and her husband moved out of the area and became patients of our friends, we all stayed in touch.

They even helped us move in and renovate my dream beach house! After a day of hefting furniture and taking out a fireplace, I wanted to thank everyone by making my then-best attempt at Sabaluche's Onion Pie. Neither Trish nor her husband had ever had onion pie, and Trish was quick to volunteer to help in the kitchen and learn by watching me.

While I was comparing all the ways my pie *still* wasn't the same as what Sabaluche made, everyone who ate it had faces of orgasmic joy. They declared the pie was the best they'd ever eaten! "I've never had anything like that!"

That version of the pie—now about twenty years ago—had a top and bottom crust, a higher tomato sauce-to-onion ratio, and grated Pecorino Romano (never parmesan!) cheese.

Since then, Trish and Scott have had a few different versions of my onion pie, and each time they say it's even better than last time. As we were working on edits for this book, Trish was at my house, and I made an onion pie to fuel our efforts. This pie only had a bottom crust, had a higher onion-to-tomato sauce ratio, and used chunks of Pecorino Romano cheese.

Trish declared this was the best yet, and in particular, best for her because she's had to lower her carbs and acid intake.

I sent slices home for her husband, too—as any good Italian mom would!

The very next day, Trish texted me: "Scott also says this is the best version yet. AND that it's still better than the ones I try to make!!!"

Have you ever worked hard to make some meal or treat for your child that a grandparent made? You collected the same exact ingredients, followed every step perfectly, and then the child declares, "Grandma's version is the best."

Frustrating, right?

I could never replicate Sabaluche's Gavadeel exactly, so I made my Patti version with butter and sage. Yet how long have I (and my family) frustrated ourselves trying to "perfect" *Sabaluche's* onion pie?

Every version of onion pie I've made was the *perfect* version I needed to make when I made it, with the ingredients I had when I made it, and for the people I wanted to nourish with it.

I'm still "perfecting" the recipe for who Patti is, and that's perfectly fine. In fact, that fits perfectly with the antithesis I've created to replace Perfect Patti: I'm now Patti Perfect.

Patti Perfect is the embodiment of the best I can be for the person I am at this time. Patti Perfect is always a work in progress, and that's exactly who she needs to be. She makes the best decisions she can with the experience, information, and emotional state she's in, and she loves her earlier versions not *in spite of* the mistakes they made (they didn't have the information she has now) but *for* the mistakes they made. After all, those mistakes allowed her to learn and continue to become a better person.

And still, if I'm being authentic—which I do strive to do now—Patti Perfect still loses her temper, gets frustrated, fails, and sometimes beats herself up for not being Perfect Patti.

Of all the "secrets" I'm sharing here, I hope you don't miss this big one: You gotta have a sense of humor, not take yourself so seriously, and let yourself have fun on this journey.

In growing yourself and raising your children, you're going to encounter things that will never, ever make sense; situations that are absolutely ludicrous and bizarre; moments that are so absurd you have to not just laugh but laugh *and* cry. In fact, in some of those situations where you just want to scream and cry, try bursting out into uncontrolled laughter. At the *very* least, you'll probably confuse your kids (and likely your partner), but there's a good chance it'll make them stop and shut up for a moment or three while they wonder if you've finally utterly and completely lost it.

Full disclosure, the last big secret: It's a *lot* of work, but it *is* worth it. Becoming your true self *and* raising children. If you want to raise children who will become the best versions of themselves, you need to model what that looks like. How can they know what they should strive to be if they don't see it in you? How can they be assured that they will get through the difficult and painful parts of growing if they don't see you struggle, fail, and get back up? How will they know it's alright to learn something that refines and changes how they define themselves if they don't see you also regularly checking in with who you are *authentically*?

And guess what: Even though the chef is growing, the recipe stays the same!

Have (and evaluate) your own personal philosophy on life, and let it be your map as you navigate this combined journey.

Follow your intuition. Learn to listen to that little voice in your heart; it will always be in tune with your most authentic self.

Love unconditionally—and that means *yourself* as well as your partner, kids, family, and whoever else you choose to love. You deserve to have your needs met as much as those you love do. You deserve to be cared for and nourished. You also deserve the space, safety, and opportunity to confront challenges and trauma that *keep* you from being your true self, your *whole* self.

If your children don't see you taking care of yourself, what are they learning about how they should care for themselves? Model the love you know *they* deserve by treating yourself with that same love.

Our children feel our true essence. They know when we are being authentic and not, and they *still* love us unconditionally if we have modeled that for them. They will be their best selves if we have modeled that for them. And most of all, they will take our recipe and add their own "flair" to it because we modeled that for them, too.

The biggest secret to this recipe is *you.* The chef.

All the experience you've had, all the people who've influenced you, and all the things that make your essence uniquely *you* are what will make your application of a deceptively simple recipe yours and yours alone. My grandmother knew intuitively that we would be eating her onion pie for generations, and we would think of her. Her legacy would live on.

What is *your* "perfect," your *best* version of this recipe? That answer is whatever the best version of *you* is whenever you're using it.

As I've been saying, this recipe is as versatile as it is simple. Change it to fit your needs—in this moment and as your needs change while you and your family *all* grow to become your best perfectly imperfect, loving, kind, and confident selves.

Four Generations of Feisty Women
Katie (1 month), Patti (34), Ceal (58), and Sabaluche (87)

I love this picture with my daughter, my mom, and my
grandmother. The bookends—Katie and Sabaluche —seem
to be having a similar experience by the looks on their faces.
Sabaluche never liked her picture taken.

Coffee Break

Serving My Parents *My* Pasta Sauce!

*"A recipe has no soul.
You, as the cook, must bring soul to the recipe."*

- Thomas Keller

My next chapter gets a little heavy as I talk about my parents aging and my father passing, so I wanted to give you the much more light-hearted Real Life reaction my parents had when I introduced them to my sage butter sauce for the first time as an appetizer.

***

It was 2013, and we were celebrating my mom and dad's sixty-fifth wedding anniversary, my sixtieth birthday, and Peter's and my thirtieth anniversary. Eleven of us family members travelled to Italy and rented a villa in Bagni di Luca for a magical week filled with many memories. The absolute best memory for me was the dinner my sister Linda and I prepared in the amazing kitchen of this villa.

My sister and I went to the market and bought the last couple of bronzini—the Italian plural name for European sea bass others might better know as "branzino." We could have

used a few more, but we made do. I volunteered to make pasta since we did have to feed all of us, and what I made turned out to be the precursor to my famous Gavadeel with Sage Butter sauce. (At the time, I'd made it with gnocchi.)

While we were growing up, Mom could always just whip together a fantastic meal—a veritable feast—at a moment's notice. Whether a relative or friend stopped in unexpectedly or it was a planned family holiday dinner, Mom was ready. And she never complained! She, like her mother, Sabaluche, took pride in serving people and having "company" in the house.

Both my sisters and I have followed that tradition, and cooking that particular dinner was an extra-special occasion.

Did I mention this villa was a-*freaking*-mazing?!

I was so excited to be cooking in this kitchen. It reminded me of the movie *Under the Tuscan Sun*. The villa had a garden terrace off the kitchen full of herbs—and lots of sage. Perfect! On *another* terrace was the vegetable garden with tons of zucchini flowers and the biggest figs I'd ever seen hanging from giant fig trees. We had all the makings for a delicious dinner and dessert!

Linda made the most incredible mozzarella-and-ricotta stuffed zucchini flowers and lathered the bronzini with the wonderful garden herbs. I made the soon-to-be famous sage butter sauce and added it to the gnocchi (not the Gavadeel this time).

I was a little nervous making a dish I had never made before—

Yes, you read that right. I had this *Holy shit!* cooking revelation that I keep mentioning only eleven years before this book's publication! There's a reason I keep reiterating that the parenting journey is *always* full of learning experiences.

So, here I was making a butter-sage sauce *for the first time* for my parents who were used to tomato sauce. Damn right I was nervous! But a part of me was as excited as a little kid to offer this meal as a present to my family for coming to Italy with us.

By dinner's end, I was shocked and delighted when the giant—and I mean *giant!*—bowl of at least six pounds of gnocchi with sage butter sauce was empty. And everyone was asking for more! Even my parents!

My mother said, "I never would have thought to make this. It is amazing and delicious!"

I was in a state of bliss. *"They liked it! They liked it!"* was singing through my head.

And I thought of Sabaluche rolling in her grave.

Chapter Thirteen

Parenting the Parents

*"To care for those who once cared for us
is one of the highest honors."*

- Peggy Speers and Tia Walker, *The Inspired
Caregiver: Finding Joy While Caring for Those You
Love*

Some years ago, in what I thought would be the final weeks that I was putting this book together, my life took a turn. My ninety-one-year-old father's nephrologist in New Jersey called me, Dad's health proxy in Boston, because his kidneys were failing and he was not a candidate for dialysis. At the time, my father had already been diagnosed with cancer and congestive heart failure; he was still recovering from a heart attack thirteen months prior.

Heart in my stomach, I gunned it from Boston to New Jersey. Let's not bring up the relationship between my foot, the gas pedal, and speed limits even on good days.

It was a *Holy shit!* moment for sure.

For better and for worse, my life and who I am had been shaped by the decisions my parents had made caring for me. My life's philosophy was built from the foundation they had taught me. The recipe I use to nourish my family—metaphorically and literally—this recipe I'm sharing with you, is my adaptation of what they passed to me.

These people now needed *me*—decades after I'd flown from their nest to make my own way in the world—to help *them* with life and end-of-life decisions!

Many of us will face this journey at some point. Some will care for a parent with a neurodegenerative disorder like Alzheimer's Disease, which causes them to lose their memories and sense of self, becoming completely dependent on us. Others will tend to frail and aging parents whose needs differ in innumerable ways. My parents, thus far, had lived healthy, vibrant lives—always proactive with their health choices. My father's heart attack was the first crisis my siblings and I had to face in our parents' later years. And now this kidney failure.

I might have finished the labor-intensive, dependent years of parenting my own children—some parents find themselves still raising young children, while caring for their aging parents!—but now I was plunged into a new parenting stage.

The life cycle is brutal like that.

I remember thinking, as I drove as fast as I could (within the speed limit of course), from Boston to New Jersey, "One day, Katie and Christopher may have to do this for me. Will they know what I want? Will they respect my philosophy and the choices I would make?"

On this drive, I also started plans for a family reunion that had to look completely natural and unrelated to Dad's health because while he would want to see as much of the family for possibly the last time, he would *hate* to think we planned an event *for* him to do this.

And we could not let on to my mom that he was closer to death, but I'll get to that.

But let me back up to before this fateful, white-knuckled exercise of my excellent driving talents. This wasn't my *first* time with "parental" responsibilities for my parents.

***

Fortunately, my father's heart attack had happened in Boston thirteen months prior. I could be present as his health proxy as we made decisions about medications and procedures.

It was quite remarkable that this was my dad's first major

experience with medications. Vitamins had been his go-to, but they weren't enough now. He needed medications to survive the cardiac arrest, yet he was cautious and told the doctors he wanted to get off the drugs as quickly as possible. He met with resistance, but I was there—his daughter, a doctor herself—to explain things to him and to his attending physicians as we made a care plan.

Like when raising my children, I was not and am not alone in caring for my parents.

Our family, my siblings, our spouses, and our children all rallied to ensure Dad received the care that best honored what he wanted for his life and body. As I mentioned, we had an unconventional upbringing with regular visits to chiropractors and learning to let our bodies heal themselves. We are an unusual family in that we question medical protocols and research before blindly accepting doctors' recommendations. I am fortunate to have an in-depth knowledge of human physiology from my Doctorate in Chiropractic, and my sisters, my brother, and other family members are excellent at investigating the pros and the cons of particular procedures or medications. We are a team, and we readily advocate for ourselves and for each other. And that was exactly what my father needed.

Besides my siblings and family, another angel was drawn to help us.

Dr. C.* was on sabbatical at Beth Israel Hospital in Boston, doing research, and happened to be checking in on residents in the ward where my father was. Intrigued by my father's outlook—that he didn't want medication and couldn't have surgery—he chose to take him on as a patient.

I distinctly remember the conversation where he very calmly told my dad, "You could die if I took you off all the medications right now."

Just as respectfully, my dad replied, "I understand, but I will not stay on medications for the rest of my life either, because the medications could very well kill me before my time. I would like you to help me do this."

Dr. C. agreed to his request, and they even shook on it. He promised to work with us to reduce the medications as long as he saw positive test results. Dr. C. even gave me his cell number to call whenever we needed him. He remained a faithful ally and stayed in touch up to Dad's passing a year and a half later in New Jersey. When I would call him to share the final news, he was deeply moved.

While we cared for our father and even after his passing, my sister, Linda, his backup health proxy, and I had many conversations about how he would probably not have survived as long as he did after his heart attack if he didn't have us (and Dr. C) advocating for him. We talked about how most patients, especially in the later years of life, just accept the doctors' recommendations without someone advocating for them. Had my father followed all the orders he'd been given after the heart attack, his body that had spent a lifetime without alcohol, drugs, or medications would have reacted poorly to what he was being prescribed. We've had friends and family members injured by doctors' well meaning recommendations that didn't work for their body. I'm not disrespecting doctors in any way, but unfortunately, we have learned that one size does not fit all when it comes to medical procedures and medications.

After his almost-fatal heart attack, Dad was in the Boston hospital for a week or so and then came to stay with Peter and me in our Westwood home. Our daughter, Katie was getting married in less than a month, and we all agreed it was best for Mom and Dad to stay with us until then. After the wedding, my sister and brother-in-law, Terry and Doug, would take over and drive my parents back to New Jersey.

During his month with us, I became Dad's "parent," monitoring his food intake.

"Why didn't you put the extra food on the table?" he'd regularly ask.

To which I always replied, "I filled all our plates with what we are going to eat. It's easier for me that way."

He lost ten pounds out of the forty-plus that he needed to drop under my dinner regimen. And the rest of us were all happy to have looser pants.

While they were at our house, Christopher and Katie visited Grandpa and Grandma often. I was impressed with our kids' care, concern, and compassion. It gave me confidence to know they would be there for Peter or me if or when they needed to care for us.

The next big *parenting the parents* discussion with my siblings was about our parents' care in New Jersey. They would need help. Mom could not do it all and we'd noticed her short-term memory was being challenged. We set our team research to finding exactly the right caretaker for our family.[13]

Of course, we needed to convince our parents they *needed* outside help.

"Mom, Dad needs help in the first two weeks of coming home, so we need your help hiring someone," one of us, probably me, pitched to her.

"I don't want some stranger living in my house!"

"No worries, Mom. She'll come in the morning when Dad wakes up, check on him, and leave after dinner. You will be in charge. She'll even help around the house with whatever you need."

"Oh, well... okay," my mother relented. "If it's only or a couple weeks."

Dad was a little easier to convince since he was already certain this would be temporary and he'd fully recover from his heart attack. Determined to get his body as strong and healthy as possible, armed with his own research on his condition, he maintained a hopeful and (rather surprisingly) compliant attitude for much of his early care decisions.

Fortunately, our first applicant was wonderful! Neither of my parents had a complaint; they were getting spoiled. Mom was especially pleased to have someone else cooking and cleaning for her. A "couple weeks" became almost a year, and then we hit another hurdle.

They needed more help on the weekends. We hired a weekend person, but then Mom also needed help putting Dad to bed at night, so our weekend person became the weekend and evening person. Eventually, problems arose between which caretaker was responsible for which duties, and dealing with *that* fell on me. (Thank you, God, for thinking I'm so strong and capable, but *really*?) In short, our weekend caretaker, Kathy, became our new fulltime caretaker. We appreciate everyone who went above and beyond to help, but Kathy stayed with my parents to our father's end and beyond—and for her dedication, we're especially grateful!

****

I mentioned not letting my mom know how close Dad was to death as I made family reunion plans during that jaw-clenching trip from Boston to New Jersey after the nephrologist's call. When you're caring for your parents, if you're fortunate enough to have both of them in your life for many years, you'll see another similarity to parenting your children.

Like each of your children are unique persons with unique needs, so are your parents. They may have chosen to spend their lives together as opposed to having *been chosen* (biologically or otherwise), like your kids were, but I can promise you that makes little difference. You still need to address each of their needs individually—and yes, intuition, philosophy, and unconditional love is the best recipe for that, too.

***

As my father adjusted to post-heart attack life, mom's short-term memory was getting worse. And as her memory got worse, Dad was having fewer conversations with her and more with the caretakers and other visitors. He wasn't conscious how his actions affected her, but Mom's behavior was showing that she felt left out.

Mom was acting more and more childlike. She would get mad over the littlest thing, and then run to her room and slam the door. Even prior to her forgetfulness, Mom had never truly figured out how to express her feelings in a constructive and rational way.

It was challenging for me (and my siblings). The signs of dementia were getting more obvious. Prior to getting caretakers, Mom was cooking pasta every night and forgetting things my dad was asking her to do.

We had to keep reminding my father not to yell at Mom. We would hear him say things like, "Ceal, I just told you that!" or "Ceal, you were supposed to do that," or "Ceal, why did you say that?"

It was horrible for me, personally, for a few reasons. First, I began to wonder if I was getting dementia, since my husband would tell me or ask me things and I would forget. (Though my kids do that too, and they are very young...) Second, I felt sorry for how mean my dad was being. I thought about how Sabaluche berated Mom, made her feel like she was always wrong, and here she was getting the same treatment from her husband of seventy years. It was not okay with me (or my siblings).

We took turns explaining, in some form or another: "Dad, please don't yell at mom when she forgets. Please talk to her more and involve her in your activities. She is feeling left out and does not know how to express it except to get angry and isolate herself in another room. That's not healthy for her or you."

We talked to the caretakers, as well. They tried their best to involve Mom, but it was more challenging as Dad's health declined.

We had to take action. We found a counselor who came to the house and gave us tips on how to communicate with someone with dementia. He told us to never make them feel wrong and don't remind them they are forgetting. That was especially hard for my dad, who was used to Mom taking care of him.

Mom started to withdraw. She spent more time on the computer than ever before, and we were getting worried. When friends and family went to visit, we had to stay cognizant of giving Mom attention. Just like a child, she would act out if we didn't. I was reminded of my own kids' tantrums when they wanted my attention when I was on the phone or socializing with a friend. I learned very quickly that the skillset I used for my kids was the same as I needed to parent my parents. So, your kids will help prepare you for those later years.

***

While my parents were home in New Jersey during my dad's recovery, part of their caretakers' responsibilities were to send me my dad's vitals every day and report what he'd taken for medicine and vitamins. We had a great system. With all Dad's documented daily vitals, four months later, he returned to Boston to see Dr. C. for a heart check-up. This was to be his final meeting with Dr. C., who was finishing his sabbatical. The tests on his heart plus the day-to-day data revealed he was doing to decrease his meds from nine to three.

Holy Shit!

Dr. C was amazed at Dad's recovery from his heart attack at the age of ninety. When Dad returned to NJ, he visited his local cardiologist, Dr. O.* who updated his chart regarding his progress and reduction of medications per Dr. C.

I continued to monitor Dad's vitals on a daily basis from Boston and regulated his medications per instructions from Dr. O., who explained, "Patti, the key is to 'keep his heart dry and his kidneys wet.' That is impossible for me to do on a day-to-day basis. But there is a bit of juggling you can safely do with the Lasix."[14] (Lasix, or furosemide, is a common diuretic prescribed to people with congestive heart failure and kidney issues.) "One of your indicators to reduce the Lasix will be swelling, mostly in his ankles and feet. If you need my assistance, please do not hesitate to call my office."

True to his word, Dr. O. was very helpful. Either he or his staff responded within twenty-four hours if I had a question or a concern. My dad had a lot of angels watching over him!

The caretakers checked his feet every day to let me know if they were swollen. I successfully adjusted his Lasix until eighteen months later, when his heart and kidneys had declined to the point of that fateful call from the nephrologist.

And my frantic drive from Boston to New Jersey.

***

Back to me responsibly following traffic laws from Boston to New Jersey while my mind raced between planning for my father's final care, wondering how my kids will care for me when I'm nearing my end, and also figuring out how to throw together a surprise family reunion for my dad in a way he would appreciate.

If the nephrologist was right in telling me my dad was in the last stages of kidney failure, I wanted us to all be together and have a chance to celebrate my dad's life. My dad loved his family, parties, and our family reunions, and we all needed to say our goodbyes in our own ways.

It was shortly before Labor Day, and the drive was full of stop-and-go traffic—which I absolutely *hated* under normal circumstances. I arrived in New Jersey frustrated and stressed to the max. And now there was work to do.

I called the siblings with the news and so they could help me come up with a story about why we were having a family reunion on such short notice. My siblings all agreed that we not make a big deal about it. We'd tell our parents that it had been a long time since such an event and just invite people over for Labor Day weekend—well, the weekend before because traffic was *already* awful.

My father was excited.

My mom...well, she has a phrase—"Did. Done. Don't Wanna."— for the instances where she may be asked to cook for a crowd, host a party, do the dishes, and the list goes on. When we mentioned a party at her house, she was perturbed and repeated this phrase as she argued, "Why do we need to do this last minute? Why didn't you ask us before making plans?"

We took it in stride and hugged her, said it would be fun, and we promised we'd do all the work. What she didn't realize was she hadn't cooked or cleaned for the past year, and we would be doing everything because we knew she couldn't. It wasn't until we mentioned that her grandkids were coming that her mood began to change.

The party happened according to plan, and it was great fun!

Some of our cousins, our only surviving aunt, Auntie Madeline, and some of the grandkids all attended this one-day eating fest! Everyone brought food on top of what my siblings and I cooked, and in the end, we had our family get-together with all our customary Italian favorites: Gavadeel and broccoli; Eggplant Parmigiana; sausage, peppers, and onions... (In case you are wondering, no Gavadeel with sage butter sauce, but if you read the last "Coffee Break," you were served that special story!)

Both my parents did great and were in ecstasy during the whole affair!

***

A few weeks after our grand reunion, we had to start hospice care for my dad.

We called the counselor who'd helped us with Mom to give us pointers about communicating this to my parents. In the end, we decided to not inform my dad or my mom that all the "extra help" they were getting was hospice care.

Wait, what?

You might be wondering, especially if you read my feelings about lying in prior chapters, how could I *not* tell my parents such a big thing? How did the choice to lie—and even the choice to readily accept hospice care—fit into my philosophy, one of the major ingredients of my recipe? Or even as part of intuition and unconditional love?

Believe me, I had all those questions too! But also, if you remember from my decision to not only have my children at home but to do it in water baths—an idea I initially thought was *crazy*—at the core of my philosophy is the importance of educating myself for every decision. And you may be surprised, as I and my siblings certainly were, that hospice was *not at all* what I'd initially thought it was. Many people, in fact, don't really understand what "hospice" entails if they've never experienced it.

Many people, myself and my siblings included before we learned better, think that hospice is someone coming with morphine and drugging a patient until they die. Just short of straight-up euthanizing a person. What I learned and passed onto my siblings is that hospice comes in to support the patient, as well as the family, so their loved one can have a better quality of life when there is nothing else available for treatment or a person chooses to forego any more medical treatment. Not only does hospice provide medical and medicinal options for comfort, but they have social workers, chaplains of various faiths, and counselors who work with all members of the family during this time, not just their patient.

I knew in my heart—guided by my intuition and the unconditional love for my parents—that no matter what research we presented to them, my parents would not be convinced "hospice" meant anything other than a death warrant. When Dad's cardiologist had told him at an earlier appointment that *his* father had been on hospice for two years, and it had improved his quality of life, my dad had rejected the option for himself because it "didn't sit well" with him.

But didn't they have a right to know? Shouldn't they be able to consent?

That's also a tricky point—also related to parenting children. Have you ever had to make a choice for your child, not telling them all the details, because the added information would only confuse them or cause them to behave in manner where they might hurt themselves or others? I've had to, and I've wrestled with that choice every time. But kids—especially when they're younger—haven't yet developed the emotional or mental capacity to be able to make certain decisions. That's why they need parents.

And as we get older, our brains can *lose* that capacity. Remember how I described my mother as childlike? That's a common descriptor for people in certain stages of Alzheimer's, dementia, and other conditions for a reason.

I was health proxy for both my parents. If my dad did not have the capacity to make good health decisions for himself, the responsibility fell on me, not my mom. I've already mentioned my mother was suffering from symptoms of dementia, which impaired her ability to make decisions. But if you're a stubborn, ninety-one-year-old Italian man willing to debate with doctors about medicine, how mentally or emotionally capable would you be when faced with your actual mortality?

Honestly, how mentally or emotionally capable are *most people* when faced with their death or the death of a loved one?

Not very, I'd wager. The fact that my father's cardiologist and all the hospice workers were willing to keep why they were there from my parents certainly suggests that we weren't the first to make this request.

My mom, for her part, was very happy to be in a state of denial. (I think I got that trait from her!) As Dad's health declined further, Mom retreated. Doing word books and playing computer mah-jong, as well as her favorite game, Rummikub, were her go-tos when not involved in a conversation or when she did not want to be social. It was a big personality change for our mom, but also not uncommon for her condition.

Hospice was a lifesaver. I know it sounds like those words don't belong together, but they do.

Hospice sent Joe, their Italian chaplain who was very personable, to visit my parents. Being Catholic church-goers, my parents could relate to him, and he quickly endeared himself to them. A hospice social worker spoke with me and my siblings at various times, as well as my parents—singly and together. The entire staff of nurses and other palliative care providers allowed our family to ease into the inevitable.

My dad wanted no heroic interventions, and they honored that.

My father had made it very clear that he wanted to stay at home with his family, regardless of what happened. He did say to me, quite humorously, when we were discussing his DNR (do not resuscitate) document, "If I am still warm, don't let them bury me."

I promised I wouldn't, and we had a good laugh.

Holding onto happy memories, laughing over dark jokes are touchstones that helped as I was going through the stress and emotional weight of watching my dad's failing health in his last three months. They grounded me as I waded through the hard decisions of what I knew he wanted for his end-of-life care, even if they sometimes didn't fit into my philosophy or beliefs.

We were blessed that our dad had been very clear with his desires to avoid any possibility of disagreement from either our mom or us siblings. Hell, he had a *five-page, handwritten document* outlining his requests for his funeral and burial—right down to who he wanted for pall bearers and who would do the eulogy. And he reminded us that he'd gotten insurance to pay for transporting him up to seventy-five miles to the funeral home. In fact, he'd suggested (jokingly) that upon his passing we put him in the car and drive exactly seventy-five miles from the funeral home so he would get his money's worth!

My siblings and I had a lot of fun conjuring up scenarios as to where to bring him and what he would be wearing when the funeral director came to pick him up in another state.

But reality check, how *would* we deal with his death at home?

I had never done this before and I was feeling ill-prepared—sort of like when I gave birth the first time. I had a lot of questions, and researching for those was not the happy exercise of preparing to birth our children. I don't think my siblings or I discussed exactly what we would do when Dad breathed his last breath, but we prepared in each our own ways. Somewhat more similar to my first birth, there were certain details we would have to figure out when it occurred, and it would be what it would be.

While we were wrestling with these questions and details, a friend suggested I read a book that she had just completed prior to her mom passing, *Being Mortal*, by Atul Guwandi, a medical physician from Boston. After reading it, I suggested it to my other family members. The book addresses end-of-life conversations that are not easy to have and are not typically suggested by physicians. The book opened my eyes to the questions to discuss and the necessity to have honest and open conversations between doctors, their patients, and patient family members regarding end-of-life options.

***

How do you care for a parent at end of life when you have to act in a way your parents would want, even though it's contrary to your philosophy?

We need to have those conversations with our parents (and our children) earlier rather than later. We don't always see the end coming. We can't always anticipate the moments that lie ahead. For them or for us. It's brutal, but it's true.

What's the best way to respect a person who changed your diapers while you might be changing theirs? How do you treat them with the dignity and care they deserve in their time of need? How do we model the dignity and care we will need when our kids may be changing our diapers?

I can't speak to every parent-child relationship; each one is different. I also can't speak to every family's ability to provide end-of-life care to their parents. What I can say is you do need to prepare yourself and your family as thoroughly as possible for the emotional, practical, financial, and spiritual work of your parent's passing—and yours.

How?

First, reread those questions I posed above. Don't shy away from them; don't pretend it won't happen. Then tune back in to that recipe of intuition, philosophy, and unconditional love. How did your parents use that recipe? How does yours differ—and even when it differs, how does yours guide you to navigate that difference?

In addition to your recipe, you also need communication. *Clear* communication. Put together a living will for yourself, a life and death plan that is *in writing.* If you already have this, great! Is it updated? Even if it is fastidiously kept up to today—in which case, I tip my hat to you!—use updating it as an excuse to ask your parents about their will and final plans.

This is one of those opportunities to teach by example—for both your kids *and* your parents if they need it. If your parents see you preparing your kids, hear you explain why you find that important, that could motivate them to make sure their plans are in place. If you're speaking with your parents about end-of-life care and final preparations, your children can see you modelling how you'd like them to care for you.

That's what I did as I was caring for my dad. My hopes were that my children, if Peter was not around or unable to make decisions, would model my behavior as they watched me help my parents through my dad's heart attack and up to his last breath. Not just my children, but my siblings, nieces, and nephews—I tried to be very conscious that my actions would inform them when they were in a situation to parent their parents.

We must also care for ourselves. Remember my recipe—including and especially the unconditional love—is important to apply to our nourishment and well-being too. Grief is a process that we need to respect.

And, like parenting our kids, shit goes wrong when we care for our parents too. I have found that sometimes, when the care methods our parents taught us are delivered back to them in their twilight years, they aren't always amenable to it. So there is a tightrope that exists between doing what you need to do and doing what they would have wanted you to do in that moment. It is a challenging situation to be in. And it will be challenging for my children.

I know some of you are squirming uncomfortably as you read this. What I'm talking about is not easy; believe me, I know. Remember how I asked how many people are emotionally capable of making decisions when faced with mortality? I, for one, used to have panic attacks as a little girl thinking about death, so it's not a subject that I like talking about. But after my experience with my dad, I am more open to having the conversation.

So what have I done so far? Am I living true to the words I'm suggesting to you?

I did mention I was still an imperfect human once or twice in this book so far. Unfortunately, at the time I'm publishing this book, I still haven't written down my end of life desires, but when I do I will reread *Being Mortal*, by Atul Guwandi, and take my friend and editor Trish's advice and read the book, *Fuck, I'm Dead Now What?* Trish also referred me to the Order of the Good Death website, which I found fascinating. From the little that I read, I like the fact that they are very open and candid about all aspects of death and dying.

But I have talked to Katie about being my health proxy after Peter. She is the oldest, and we've had some deep philosophical conversations over the past few years about life, death, how to care for our health, and how I would want someone to care for me at the end of my life. She understood I wanted to be cared for like I cared for my father: at home and no heroic efforts.

These aren't conversations I've had with my son, though. Christopher tends to shy away from challenging and emotional conversations. I know this because I know him. Case in point: During one of the more "colorful" kitchen discussions between Katie and me, Peter walked into the living room area by our open kitchen, where our son was reading a book, and asked, "Christopher, do you know what is going on with your mom and Katie?"

"I don't know, Dad," he answered. "I just know it's much safer in here".

Katie's health care choices are in alignment with Peter and me—another reason for asking her. I remember during 2020, when I was grappling with health care decisions regarding Covid, I asked Katie for her opinion. Her answer was exactly what I would do.

In regard to honoring whatever I chose for my end-of-life plans, she agreed to do so but insisted on one big thing.

"Mom, I need you to write it down. Everything you want me to do. So I know exactly what you want, and so Christopher will know too."

Just as I would expect from my Katie. And I know Christopher would have requested that too. And I *will* have a conversation with Christopher about our end-of-life desires at some point in the future, when appropriate for the occasion.

Even though I still have work to do, I trust my children will do right for us. They both regularly visited their grandpa at the hospital several times. When my parents were staying with Peter and me, they came to the house often. And it always cheered my parents up. They watched as I travelled to NJ a couple weekends a month, and they and their spouses all attended that last family reunion with Grandpa before his passing. I was grateful for how they showed up for Grandpa and Grandma—playing Rummikub with my mom for hours!—and for how they showed up for me. Attentive to my needs, they both promised, "Mom, we are here for you. Just ask."

And I did remember to ask, and they were there, as promised. I was so proud of both of them. Pardon me…I still need a tissue.

***

Don't judge yourself in the moments when you are second guessing your parent's wishes. Another reason for having a living will and other documents with end-of-life wishes is to help you navigate the difficult decisions. When directions are there, written in black and white, they are a gift to your mind and soul because you don't have to *think*—and believe me, when you're worried about someone you love, when you're carrying that much fear and grief, *thinking* is not exactly easy. The fact is you never know what you must do, what you will do, or what you are able to do until the moment is right there in front of you. You do your best to make the appropriate decision. Use the recipe: trust your intuition, act in alignment with your parents' values as expressed by them, and proceed with loving care, kindness, and unconditional love.

The same goes for your children when the time comes for them to parent you and make end-of-life decisions for you. Yes, prepare them to the best of your ability—in fact, giving clear instructions lets them authentically experience their emotions without the burden of having to think or guess in making certain decisions—but understand they will be struggling and hurting no matter what. Lessen that as much as you can. If you've shared the recipe of intuition, philosophy, and unconditional love—which I hope you do as my family shared it with me—you all will be better capable of nourishing and caring for each other even in most difficult times.

If I haven't made it clear, I *continue* to learn and adapt my recipe for my family's needs. And I will still be learning, even if or when there comes a time I can't putter around an actual kitchen.

I remember sitting on the bed with my dad two days before he died, holding his hand and being a goofball, as I am known to do. I made some kind of joke.

He looked at me the way he did when I was doing something he *didn't* think was funny. "Patricia, you can leave now."

Then we laughed.

The next day, when I was holding his hand, I said, "I love you, Dad."

He was fading in and out of consciousness. Though he had difficulty getting the words out, he managed, "Thank you for all you have done for me."

I cried!

Those were his last words to me. He died peacefully in bed the day after, just as he wished.

Mom was in the kitchen when he took his last breath.

I went out and told her he was gone and hugged her. She was frantic and wanted to know if we could do something to bring him back.

At that very moment, Aunt Vera, our parents' closest friend arrived with her granddaughter. We gave her the news. She went over, took my mother's hand, and they both sat by my father's bedside. We lined up chairs so they could sit comfortably and comfort each other.

My siblings and I floated in and out of the room, checking in and grieving at the sight of our dad, gone from his physical body. His body remained there for a few hours before we called the funeral home.

No, we didn't put him in a car and drive him seventy-five miles away. But we thought about it!

I am reliving that moment while editing this chapter and thinking about how, when I'm taking my last breath, I want to be holding the hands of my loved ones, hearing them tell me they love me. And while I'm alive and on this planet, I will take every opportunity to let my dear friends and family know I love them through my words and my actions. I'll keep cooking my famous Gavadeel (or gnocchi) with sage butter sauce and baking onion pie. It gives me joy to make it and gives me joy to hear, "That is the best pasta and pizza I have ever tasted!"

Of course it is. I made it, with love, for them, with my own special family recipe, passed down through generations *with love.*

*I'm using initials to reference the doctors for the privacy of them and their current patients.

Patti and Peter, kids grown and out of the house, are still very much in love. An intuitive spark, a philosophy shared by souls, and unconditional love personified.

Coffee Break

What Do You Feed an Empty Nest?

"When we're looking for compassion, we need someone who is deeply rooted, is able to bend and, most of all, embraces us for our strengths and struggles."

- Brené Brown

So your kids have left the house. Moved out. Gone to college, gone to live with friends or a special partner, gone traveling to pursue their heart's vocation... Now what?

My unsolicited advice—or solicited, as you *are* reading my book:

If you find yourself an empty nester and are in a state of having to get to know your spouse again, throw yourself into it, heart and soul! Find a way to renew and re-establish your relationship with this person who you chose to be your life partner. You will need each other as you navigate these new waters.

There may be some big questions looming.

Will we look at our partners at that moment and think, *"Who are you? I don't know who you are anymore..."* or will we look and think, *"Holy shit! We can be as loud as we want while making love and not have to worry about the kids hearing us..."*?

Will we have so much spare time that we feel lost or will we pack it with so much work that we can't feel the void? Will we feel blessed to have this newfound freedom or will we feel lost and unfamiliar to ourselves now that we aren't chasing babies all day?

Will we find things to talk about other than our kids? Or will we be able to let go, and as they say in these parts, *pahtee!* (sounds like "potty" when spoken like a true Bostonian)?

Relationships need everyday nurturing, and as I say this, please know that I need to get reminded of this as much as anyone. For as great as my relationship is, Peter and I have our day-to-day disagreements, struggles, and moments when we don't like each other. Our friend, Pam, has called us the "Bickersons" on more than a few occasions.

I've said it before, and I'll say it a thousand times more, Peter is my greatest supporter, my best fan, and my biggest cheerleader. I'm blessed to share my life with him. That isn't to say we don't have our challenges—especially when faced with big life changes. But we also took the time to prepare for them.

At about the ten-year mark in our marriage, Peter and I looked around at our closest, dearest friends and saw many were breaking up or having challenges in their marriages. We looked at each other and thought, "Holy Shit! We don't want that to be us!"

We dragged ourselves off to a therapist. The therapist just about laughed at us when our first disagreement in therapy was over who had it better. I thought I was the lucky one to have Peter. Peter thought he was the luckier one to have me.

If you want to gag at how great our relationship is, well, as the kids say, #sorrynotsorry. I can't and won't apologize. And I hope it offers you inspiration. I am proud of us! We are not perfect, but we vowed to always place our relationship as high priority and keep the romance alive. That has led us to success in overcoming even our greatest challenges.

And if an amazing partner is not part of your life, I'm

also proud of you for accomplishing all you've done in choosing to take the roads you've taken. It's a shit ton of work! I couldn't have done it without Peter. And I hope you have and have had other fulfilling relationships in your life that support you with the unconditional love you deserve. As I hope you personalize my parenting recipe to your needs and your life, apply my thoughts relating to my marriage as what fits your life and relationships when your children have left home to live their own lives.

While Peter and I might not have been breaking up, it's never a bad thing to build strength into your relationship—any relationship—when things are going well. Many people wait for a crisis. We see it every day in our practice as chiropractors. People blindly living their lives realize they should take action when life hits them with a cosmic two by four. They get their gym membership when they're on the verge of a heart attack, change their diet when their doctor says they're pre-diabetic.

So, just as we do positive things on a regular basis to build the wellbeing of our body rather than waiting for a symptom or a crisis to motivate us, as chiropractors and parents, Peter and I tend to follow that same philosophy in our relationship as a couple. Besides the counseling, we regularly check in on how we're feeling, as individuals and as a couple. We direct and hone our intuition, beliefs, and unconditional love toward each other. We see if those things are still resonating on the same wavelengths. We listen to ourselves and each other on that deeper level.

Besides checking in with our partners and closest relationships, it's important to check in on ourselves—and ask for help if we need it. From those close relationships, from professionals, or from other resources you trust.

When I had moments that I felt lost as a parent (or even prior to parenthood), I would seek help from a personal therapist/coach, or a psychic, or a personal development course.

I know I'm a little out there: I am just as likely to seek a spiritual healer as I am to seek help from a traditional counselor. Each one of us has got to do what is right for *us,* and for me, I like to stretch myself and see what's possible in all realms, including and especially the metaphysical.

The ability to seek out the right sort of help to find yourself when you feel lost is a skill that will help you when your kids move out of your home—and a good many other times in life. It doesn't always turn out like we thought it would, and in those times, your life partner and your village matter. Don't go it alone.

****

That moment of realization that life continues without kids at home needs to have a pause button. We should approach this new state of living with awareness of self, as well as awareness of your partner and/or other household members and/or close relations. Listen to your intuition; it will tell you what you need. Check in with your beliefs and philosophy to guide your actions. And love unconditionally— yourself, those around you, and your children in their new lives outside your home.

I believe in repeating important truths—be it about my kids, my husband, or my intent. I wrote this book and shared this recipe for others to personalize. It's great for parenting, but it's also great for *living*—however your life changes.

Even when those changes are so massive they hit your household like a mid-life crisis.

Should we buy a beach house for Patti so she can be in her happy place?

You bet! And we did. It was and still is a perfect fit: a place where I can deeply tune into my intuition through my favorite sounds, sight, smells, feels, and tastes; a place to reflect on my beliefs and have stimulating conversations about philosophy with people who I respect; a place where I can give and receive love unconditionally from friends, family, myself, and the whole universe!

Should we buy that convertible that Peter had been longing for?

Absolutely! He loves speeding down the highway and feeling the wind in his face. He has an uncanny ability to totally scare the shit out of passengers (often earning him the "Masshole driver" moniker of pride or shame, depending on who you ask) while seamlessly navigating the infamous Boston Traffic—even using the restricted breakdown lane (aka the "fast speed lane," another feature or bug unique to this area)—all while incessantly laughing his unforgettable laugh. Peter calls it creative driving; others call it insane. If you observe closely, you will realize that he is in his happy place: blasting the music, flying like the wind, and contemplating the meaning of the universe. Having fun is one of his core values. As his wife, I've learned saying anything to him about his driving will get my head bitten off. Believe me, it isn't pretty! But I love the pure joy driving his convertible gives him.

Don't discount the importance of your own fantasies and wishes, as silly or frivolous or "out there" as they may seem or others may say. You've raised amazing people who are out in the world, doing amazing things, because of the work you've put in. As proud as you are of their accomplishment, as much as you want to reward them, don't forget to be proud of *yourself* and reward *yourself.* You chose and followed a path that is certainly *not easy.* You put in all the work you did, you've given them the tools to create their best life, and now you're *letting them go to live that best life!*

It's the sweetest dessert after the greatest meal you could create—and you should enjoy it.

Chapter Fourteen

Loosening the Apron Strings:
Letting Go and Trusting the Recipe

*"Sometimes love means letting go
when you want to hold on tighter."*

- Melissa Marr

At what point do you "cut" or "loosen the apron strings"? I've heard it's when your kids finally move all their crap out of your house! If that's the case, there's a part of my kids that will never leave (both literally and metaphorically). Heck, my daughter moved out at age twenty-eight with the clothes on her back (and whatever was in her car) but left several bins in my barn until I discarded everything except a few special items.

As my husband and I were in the process of cleaning out our house for our newest adventure—moving to California to be part of Life Chiropractic College West—I found Katie's unicorn collection in one of my closets along with my son Christopher's turtle collection. I told them I wanted at least one of their collectibles for myself in my new home so I would feel their presence with me.

A part of me is unable to let go of some of their stuff, even though they are both married and have been on their own for years. So, those "apron strings" are never *really* cut at all...

Before I get into that, let me tell you what I mean when I say "loosen the apron strings." If you've stuck with me to this last chapter, you won't be surprised that I've put my own spin on that meaning.

Per my editor's explanation, which she says I should include to get everyone on the same page, this particular English idiom has changed meaning over the years and still differs regionally. The most common historical or frequently-used meaning is about a child (usually a boy) shyly or anxiously clinging to a mother's apron strings (moms usually being the ones in aprons) or a mother tying their kid to an apron string much like we sometimes see young kids leashed to parents nowadays, particularly in crowded or public places where it's easy to lose a kid prone to wandering (or for worse reasons!) There are other, more negative, meanings dating back to the Seventeenth Century—also still used today—usually directed toward men who are perceived to be closely controlled by their mother or another woman or some idea perceived as "feminine."

For my purposes, I consider the "aprons strings" a symbol of the tie between a parent and child: the influence, care, and *healthy* control a parent has as they raise and protect their kid, as well as the dependence, trust, and compliance a child has for their parent as they learn how to survive and thrive on their own. Are there less healthy, even toxic, forms of this bond? Unfortunately, yes. Since you're reading this book about my "recipe" for parenting, where I regularly reference nourishing relationships, I figure you're here for healthy reasons.

Besides my "apron strings" referencing that parent-child dependency bond, I also believe "loosening"—the child becoming an independent adult—is an act done by both parent and child. Children loosen that tie by acts of independence; parents loosen it by acts of trust.

And let me tell you, neither of those is entirely easy—but the parenting side is definitely harder!

***

I left home at the age of seventeen. I loosened the apron strings by going to college: partly to pursue my dream to become a physical education teacher, inspired by my high school gym teacher, and partly because I needed freedom from the day-to-day suppression of living in the home of my very strict and overbearing Italian parents. And I didn't go *that* far. Less than an hour away, I started a new life in a new environment with less supervision as to what I was wearing and doing.

I won't go too much into the transition away to college except to say my parents were kicking and screaming through their whole part of loosening those apron strings.

I had a goal, and I was passionate about it.

I was making a life of my own, separate from my parents, but not by shutting them completely out of my life. I still loved them and regularly visited them, attending all our family holidays. But I loved my independence, and as I found, time (and a lot of personal growth work) can really heal all wounds. (At least in circumstances like mine.)

After I graduated college, I experimented with how loose I wanted those apron strings. I moved all the way out to San Fransisco, lived there five months with my boyfriend and a roommate, realized it wasn't working out, and returned to New Jersey—but not to my parents' home! I moved in with other roommates in a town centrally located to most of my hundreds (I'm not exaggerating this number, I swear!) of other relatives. With the exception of those still in Italy, most of my family resided in New Jersey and Pennsylvania.

After a few years more, I'd begun to feel unhappy with my lack of passion for my job. I was meant to do something more to help people. Luckily, my boyfriend at the time—who would end up being the seven-year relationship I broke off when I met Peter—encouraged me to go back to school and live my dream. Inspired further by my then-chiropractor, I spoke with several women chiropractors. That's what I'd needed! At twenty-six years old, I loosened those apron strings more and headed to chiropractic school.

In Marietta, Georgia.

When I told Sabaluche where I was going, she said, "Thatsa'notha country!"

I laughed at the time. Later, I realized that she was saying I was off to a different culture, and it would take a few adjustments (no pun intended...*wink, wink*) to get used to living in the South. That was the Seventies, and it *was* very different than it is now.

Three and a half years later, months and weeks before I graduated, everyone—my parents especially—wanted to know,

"Where are you going to open up your practice?"

The Back Bay of Boston was my answer. That was where my boyfriend-turned-fiancé and I had chosen: close enough to our NJ families, yet far enough away for our independence. Sounds selfish now, as I am writing this, but it was necessary.

I graduated and prepared to move my life to Massachusetts with my fiancé, but we had two big hurdles: selling our house in Atlanta and me passing the board exam in Massachusetts. My fiancé went to deal with selling the house, and I left with two friends, who I would drop off along the way, and a trailer hitched to my truck with the intent of finding a place to live in Boston. I was going to save the world, living the life of my dreams as a chiropractor, and my fiancé, an architect, was going to make a name for himself in the Bay State.

As I grew up and became my own person, "loosening the apron strings" meant steps of letting and go and trusting...*myself.* In each of the scenarios I've shared, I made my decision from a place of trusting my gut—my intuitive sense—in alignment with my values and beliefs, and feeling my heart in total agreement—unconditional love for myself and my dreams.

When you *know* that you know something is right for you, it's a great feeling!

When it's someone else's life, future, and dreams at stake—a person you chose to bring into the world—it's fucking terrifying!

When Katie was born, I cried knowing that I (and Peter) could not protect her from all the challenges and possibilities of harm she may encounter. I renewed my faith in God and envisioned angels watching over her. As a matter of fact, as I'm redrafting this chapter for the whatever time, I had a conversation with Katie about a long drive she was going to take on her own. I was silent on the phone after she told me her friend could not go with her, and she picked up my angst.

"Mom, remember you told me that angels are with me all the time, watching over me and keeping me safe?"

Holy Shit! "I did say that!" I agreed, mostly because it made me feel better to affirm that to her. But it was really for me: to remind myself that I cannot control and oversee everything that might happen to my children.

Thank you, Katie, for continuing to be my greatest teacher and reminding me to let go and trust. And letting me know that my words have offered solace and protection.

***

Some years ago, I was giving a talk on parenting at a chiropractic seminar, and a parent came up to me after I came off the stage and asked, "At what point do you *have* to let them go?"

My answer wasn't as simple as the asker expected. I told her, "My heart's answer would be 'never,' but the reality is we bring them into the world and sculpt them into the best creation we can, so they can stand on their own two feet and be a self-sustaining force for good. And 'never' doesn't mean we can hover over them and think we have the right to control any aspect of their lives. *Never* means that they will always be in our hearts. *Never* means we will always care and love them. And *never* means we have to trust that they are making the decisions that are right for them and their family, if they have chosen that path. After all, we have to accept that no matter what, we did our best with the knowledge we had then. Now it is their turn to create their life adventures."

As I mentioned in the education chapters, *letting go* started when I was in labor. With one final push, I brought them forth into the world. I couldn't hold them inside any longer. And then *that* moment was inevitably followed by the cutting of the umbilical cord. And then trust that this baby will breathe on its own...

I still remember that moment with Katie, suspended in time, as she took what felt like an eternity to breathe. In that first moment of letting go, I met with the fear that she might not make it. But she did.

Of course, not all parents give birth. For those parents, they have that very first time holding their child—whether their child was born via Caesarian section or they'd just helped a partner give birth or they've just signed adoption paperwork. That first time holding *your* child will inevitably end.

There's the next moment of letting go: the first time someone else besides you holds your child. You have to trust they will be okay.

I was the only one to hold each of my children for nine months until Peter caught them on their way out of the birth canal. He was first to hold our babies outside of my womb, and then he gave each to me to hold, skin on skin. But then the midwife needed to measure our little creations, and the facsimiles of my heart—our hearts— were in someone else's hands.

I had to trust.

The years that follow are more little moments of surrender: the first-time home with just Daddy (or Mommy) while you go to work or school or errands; the first meal that didn't come from Mommy or that you didn't hold a bottle for. The first babysitter, first day of school, first sleepover—all these *firsts* until that giant step into a shared relationship with a special someone they want to spend their life with or deep passion they want to dedicate their life to. Trust that your parenting wisdom brought them to this place with confidence in themselves, trusting *their* intuition and *their* heart to choose their perfect partner or life path aligned with their values!

My kids went to high school in Oregon. I had to let go and trust.

Christopher graduated and went to Worcester Poly Tech, a little over an hour away in Massachusetts. He had the chance to go anywhere in the country, but he wanted to be closer to home. I was overjoyed!

After he graduated, he was blessed to be hired by the company he'd interned with. He had many offers—he'd gotten the highest honors in eighth grade—and he continued to shine in college with a double major, one in electrical engineering and the other in computer science. His girlfriend, K.*, who became his wife five years later, was already working in the same field.. He was a happy camper!

They moved in together: another level of letting go! Another woman in his life! And I thought what I think every mother thinks, *Will he forget about his mother?*

When Katie moved in with her friend, Trish, the amazing editor of this book—a safe place for her first big move away from her parents—we were empty nesters again. We had to let go of fear, trusting Katie to find her way.

While away, Katie chose to go to massage school. At first, I was worried she wouldn't be able to handle the academics, but she proved me wrong. She funded her own education working three jobs, studied incessantly, and graduated with knowledge and skills to apply to her passion for helping people. Currently, she is sought after for her talent as a masterful and award-winning massage therapist.

***

Part of letting go and accepting is realizing that it is okay to feel whatever you are feeling when the apron strings start to loosen. Your child is growing up into independence—the goal of good parenting! It might happen later than you expect. It might happen earlier. But whenever it happens, it is meant to. Listen to the little voice in your head that says, *Trust!*

Maybe you're not a parent who's worried about a child who's leaving the nest but a child who hasn't left yet. I mentioned Katie moved in with her friend, but that was in her mid-twenties. She did a lot of traveling, but did stay home for many years—before and after her time living with Trish.

You may have an adult child or two still living at home. Maybe they are still in college or maybe they graduated and want to save money before getting a place of their own. Perhaps they are married or with a partner and/or they might have kids, but they are saving up for a house. No matter what, it is normal to want to help and support while at the same time dreaming of the day you will be an "empty nester" and can sell your house and downsize.

My generation was different. We couldn't wait to move out and have our independence. Kids who remained home were unfortunately ridiculed, labeled as "mama's boys" or "spinsters"—at least in many cultures. An interesting distinction from the generation and culture of my parents, where families lived in the same neighborhood, often in two- or three-decker houses with several generations. And for my family in Italy, many relatives still live in the same town they grew up in—the same house as their parents, even—whether they are married or not.

***

My journey of trust, surrender, and letting go—of loosening those apron strings on my children—didn't stop when they moved out. Oh no! Both kids were on their way to living the life paths they were called to by following their own intuition, their own philosophies, and led by the unconditional love in their own hearts. Excellent!

(And if you are anything like me, you want your kids to be with you forever. You want to have a larger part in their lives, where they share their secrets, their challenges their joys and successes.)

But both my kids found special people with whom to share their beautiful lives—people who we, their parents, had to trust could *possibly* love, care, nurture, and support our babies as much and as well as we did! And even then, we had the responsibility as parents to respond to their choices *still* with that simple and complex recipe of intuition, our philosophy, and unconditional love.

Katie had been dating Alex for a couple of months when she came home from work—she'd moved back in when she'd gotten a massage job closer to us—and nonchalantly said, "Mom, Alex wants me to move in with him. What do you think?"

At this point in our relationship, I knew when Katie asked me a question like that, usually she'd already made up her mind and was looking for assurance and agreement that she was making the right decision. *But* if I agreed with her completely, she'd doubt herself; if I argued, she'd convince herself she's doing the right thing because it was opposite my disagreement. But there was an answer I could give that would make her feel validated and help her learn to trust her inner wisdom. I responded just as nonchalantly as she, "I don't know, Katie. What do you think?"

"I think I will," she said and headed right back out the door.

I assume she went to her new home with Alex that night because she never returned home—ever!

Two weeks later when she came to visit after seeing a massage client at her job in the next town, I asked, partly joking and partly wanting a non-intrusive way to clarify her living situation, "If you're living with Alex now, could I use your room as my office?"

Just as nonchalantly as she proposed the question to me about living with Alex, she said, "Sure, Mom."

That was it! Part of me was in shock. Another part said to myself, "You done good, and you need to trust that she is making a good decision."

Intuitively I knew Alex was a good match for her. And it was time! She was twenty-eight, and self-sufficient (mostly). I could loosen the apron strings more.

My response was a little different some years later on her wedding day. We were driving up the road to the garden where she would soon walk down the path to marry Alex, and she said, "Mom, Alex and I want Tory—" (one of their mutual friends) "—to get married with us today."

I almost shit my pants! What?! Who? Why hadn't this come up prior to this very second? I slammed on the brakes, turned from the steering wheel, and looked directly into her eyes. Very clearly and loudly, I stated, "No fucking way! This is not something you bring up within five minutes of walking down the aisle! No, Katie, I will not allow it!"

As nonchalantly as she'd asked about moving in with Alex—at least as well as I remember in the state I was in—she replied, "Okay, Mom."

A little shocked but so thankful for her response, I continued up the hill to the venue. Katie married Alex at a beautiful ceremony. As I'm writing this, they are still happily married.

In retrospect, this wedding scenario reminded me of the story I shared in a previous chapter about how I finally, in Katie's words, "let my Jersey out" and let her know, without a shadow of a doubt, what I was thinking. And she'd congratulated me for being authentic with her for what she felt was the first time. Marriage is a major decision in anyone's life. I don't know what all led up to her last-minute ask about changing plans, but if what she wanted was my authentic response, I gave it to her. It may not have been pretty, but it was exactly what my intuition, my philosophy, and my unconditional love all screamed out.

As for Christopher, I mentioned I'd had to let go and surrender, loosen the apron strings attached to him when he moved in with K. upon graduation. He didn't ask my opinion—nor did he need to—it just happened organically.

The two were perfect for each other. Both were engineers, working in similar fields, introverts, very independent, and very interested in each other. I loved seeing how they connected! They talked their own language—computer—and they loved mountain climbing, investing a lot of time and money into this hobby. They even invited Peter and me to share the experience of climbing with them— on easier trails. Both Peter and I are athletic and appreciated spending time with them, but I still prefer my biking hobby. Regardless, I'm thrilled my son found a kindred spirit who shares his passions!

Christopher and K. organized their own wedding, paid for it on their own, and I had little to no involvement in most of the planning. I have always seen, heard, and experienced that planning for a wedding can be the most stressful time in a couple's life before they are actually married. As the mother-in-law, I waited for their cues as to what they wanted from me, and as it turned out, they had everything under control. All I needed to do was show up. Initially, I felt like I was being left out, but then I realized that I probably would've done the same thing if I were in their position. They made it easy for us to enjoy the months leading up to the wedding day without feeling responsible for anything. All I had to do was show up and look beautiful! Seriously, I love and appreciate them for giving me that gift.

Now, when Peter and I were planning our wedding, we (and our parents) had only known each other for three months. Plus, we were both new in our practices and needed to keep our focus on our patients. I didn't have time to plan a wedding, so I called my mother. "Mom, can you please plan the wedding for us? Just let me know when you need me to decide on food choices."

Peter was within earshot and got very upset. "I want to pick out the colors and the flowers!"

Holy Shit! Who was this man? The men in my family had never cared about wedding plans. They were told (by the women) what to wear, usually a tux, and when to show up at the church. This man I was going to spend my life with was different. I liked it!

And now I had to convince my mother.

Rather than alleviating stress, my bright idea had made things more complicated. So I took the easy way out and let Peter handle things with my mother. It all worked out, and to this day, he calls her "his favorite mother-in-law."

Our wedding had over two hundred people. Half were relatives I hadn't seen in forever, and only twenty (per my mother's instructions) were friends. Even though my mother (with Peter) planned the wedding and my parents paid, it was still my wedding so I had to be a little radical and nonconformist. We kept secret our entrance procession song, for example. My parents expected "Ave Maria." When the opening to "Flashdance...What A Feeling," from the 1983 movie, sounded, the horror on my parents' faces was priceless. And captured in photos! Their arms locked on mine as they glared—while I dreamily stared down the aisle, mesmerized at my grinning husband-to-be—still brings me indescribable joy to this day.

Christopher and K. entirely created their own ritual of tying the knot at the altar with only sixty-five people in attendance, half of which were friends. While very different than my wedding, and Katie's garden wedding (where she and Alex danced to Tom Lehrer's "Masochism Tango"), it was just as powerful and amazing. All three were celebrations of unconditional (and unconventional) love, unique to each couple making vows.

We raised our kids to be independent, but it still can be devastating to see them leave the safety of their childhood home and start creating a life of their own, without you, the person who they used to rely on for everything: their shelter, their safety, and—whether you birthed them or chose them through adoption or other routes—their life.

Looking back, I know what became of that seventeen-year-old Jersey girl who left home for college with one dream, crossed the country to live near one boyfriend and some friends, returned to the area near home—but not her parents' home—and then went south to pursue a dream that was truer to her heart... Who left the cross-country boyfriend, found a man she might've married who urged her to follow her heart to her truest vocation, and then left that beloved man for one who resonated with her *truest* heart and *truest* self. I know who she was and who she is now, and I'm so proud of her. I love her. I also see who all her siblings are, who they've become, and I'm so proud and I love them all so much. Maybe that makes it feel like loosening the strings from my parents was easier—or maybe it was because it felt like I was the only one affected by those choices.

I didn't know what my parents were going through in their hearts.

I have some idea now. And "God bless them" is all I can say! I'm so proud of the relationship I finally found with them, and I love them so much.

***

As our kids get older, we parents have less and less control of their lives' trajectory and safety. Somewhere along the line, we must accept that loss and adapt. Some of us do; other parents try to maintain their hold and end up in an endless cycle of control and resentment.

The only way to live happy is to confront the fact that you can't control your children—at any stage of their life! You can only guide them as they discover their own intuition, advise them with your foundational philosophy until they develop their own, love them unconditionally, expose them to a reliable village of family members and friends, and (depending on your belief system) pray with all your might.

"But Patti," you might be saying, "I can't sleep some nights worrying about my kids and my grandchildren."

I hear you loud and clear!

My mother (in her mid-nineties) still tells me, "Call me when you get home."

I'm in my seventies! I used to get upset, but now I just joke or roll my eyes.

To which she responds, somewhat snarkily (clearly a trait of my family's mothers and daughters!), "Don't look at me like that. You never stop being a mother at any age!"

It's true! This recent solo road-trip was far from the first my daughter's taken. I regularly have asked for the phone number and address of the person she is going to stay with. Other times, I've bitten my tongue because I don't want to sound like my mother.

Both my kids are in their thirties now, and I still worry!

It takes some surrender to realize that you can't impose your ideals and values onto your adult kids. You can't do it with their choice of partner, or their chosen career, or how many children they have—if they have children at all.

***

Katie had given us a heads-up about the conversation topic and reason she wanted to take Peter and me out to breakfast. Even so, we were still thrown when—immediately upon all of us sitting down, I might add—she asked, "What was your purpose in having kids?"

After taking a moment to collect myself, I inquired, "Why are you asking us?"

"Alex and I had a discussion about having kids, and we could not see any purpose, so we are curious why you and Dad wanted to have kids."

WOW! I wasn't prepared for this question specifically. And honestly, I wasn't prepared to hear the conclusion of her discussion with Alex on having kids. I also felt like, if I gave the wrong answer, it would be my fault that they decided not to have kids.

Peter and I both responded, almost in unison, "I really have to think about that, Katie."

The truth is, I really *didn't* have to think about it. What I had to think about was how to say the right words with the greatest impact that expressed my deepest feelings—without it sounding lame. Overcome with emotions, memories of my obstetrics and gynecological classes in chiropractic school, and the recollection of having a baby growing inside me and giving birth, I blurted, "You know, Katie, for me, it was a deep longing I had after studying the body and learning how amazing the process of a growing a baby inside of me would be..." (Never mind the fun of getting pregnant—but I didn't say that part to her!) "Your dad and I wanted to create something beautifully and uniquely ours. We wanted to have a family that we created and to raise our children in a natural way."

As I remember, Katie was happy with my answer but was *more* interested to hear Peter's response.

His answer was similar to mine, except for the *growing the baby inside* part. Always more philosophical than I am, Peter eloquently stated, "Katie, we wanted to create a family and raise kids with our values and philosophy of life because we would be contributing something good for the future generation."

She didn't respond further to our answers but to say that she wanted to ask her grandparents (my mother and father) too.

I figured she didn't respond because she was not feeling complete with our answers alone and was still in need of more information, but I can't say for sure.

In the following few months, she visited my parents, and I happened to be there when she asked them the same question. She even recorded the conversation.

My dad was so sweet. He said, "Katie, you know, we wanted to have a family so we could have grandchildren like you and

Christopher and your cousins. We wanted to love and be loved. That's what everyone did when we were growing up. You got married, and you started a family."

My mother agreed and added, "I loved raising my kids and seeing them turn out successful. And none of them turned out to be bad people. They all have great jobs, and we have a loving family that sticks together."

I watched Katie smile at their responses.

My dad inquired why she was asking and she told them what she and Alex were trying to decide. I am not sure where the conversation went after that. I left before I heard the answer, but I hope she didn't tell my parents what she told Peter and me—that she and Alex could not see any purpose to having kids. It would have blindsided and saddened them.

I always wanted kids, and with that I just assumed that, when my kids got married, they would have kids of their own. My kids and their partners have, up to this point, shared their intentions to not have kids. I would be lying to say that I am totally fine with it.

On the other hand, I applaud that they have made a conscious decision based on their values and philosophy and not followed what society or their parents may have wanted.

My parents grew up in a generation where women stayed home and had babies. Life has changed a little. Expectations have changed a lot. It used to be Mom, Dad, and kids. These days a family can be a single parent family, two parents of the same gender, and any number of combinations.

The progression of some societal expectations *haven't* seemed to change much though.

Those without a partner in their early twenties still hear, "When will you get a boyfriend/ girlfriend?"

Once the boyfriend or girlfriend or partner is achieved, then comes, "When are you getting engaged?"

If an engagement happens, once a ring is on someone's finger, people ask, "When's the wedding?"

And then, "When are you having kids?" (Even for same-sex couples with what's available with egg implants, surrogate parents, adoption, and those options.)

Does having kids even have to be an assumed outcome? Not at all.

People ask me all the time, "When will you have grandchildren?"

The answer is, "Maybe never."

Many parents comfort themselves with the knowledge that grandchildren might fill the void left behind when their babies fly from the nest. But the world is changing: The ideal family looks different now. Some people feel strongly that children aren't in their plan, and that there are other ways to leave a legacy. Some believe the world has enough people in it already or they just don't see a purpose in their life to have kids.

That is okay! You aren't a failure if your child isn't going to give you grandchildren. Your kids will contribute to society! It doesn't have to look the way it always used to.

I may not have grandchildren, but I do have a grand-dog and two grand-cats. I also have chiro-babies and grandbabies from other chiropractors. Several families who've been part of our practice for generations have made Peter and me "adopted grandparents." *And* I have two great-grandbabies from my chiro-grandkid whose parents are my friends and chiropractic colleagues. They are an integral part of my life and allow me the honor to be a grandma to their kids.

Even if I didn't have those things, my parenting journey was still worth it. Christopher and Katie were a match made in Heaven for Peter and me, and there are a billion ways to leave a legacy.

Would I do it all over again?

I don't know. Maybe I would, maybe I wouldn't—

Oh, who am I trying to kid? "What was I thinking?" Yes of course I would!

And, honestly, we can never tell what we would have done differently if we had chosen a different road, but I know this: I love my kids with all of my heart and know that the world is a better place because they are in it. Grandchildren or not!

***

My parenting journey has included many—*many, many*—lessons in letting go and trusting. I not only learned, but often had to *re*learn to trust myself and my children.

I strove to be the example of the person I wanted my kids to be: someone who trusted (there's that word again!) intuition, who had a clear philosophy and guiding beliefs, and who loved unconditionally.

And in return, *they* helped *me* listen to my gut, be authentic to my beliefs, and *truly* know what it means to love unconditionally—*myself* as well as others.

In the end, all we can do is do our best. We cannot force our children to be anything that is not part of who their essence is. We can only be an example and model of how to authentically live our own lives, and they can either adopt or reject the beliefs, values, and philosophies that are part of our essence.

And we *must* do this with unconditional love. And then trust the outcome.

One day I will *cut* the apron strings and pass on to the next realm of my existence. When I do, I want my kids to know I loved them and appreciated them every day. I worked hard to be the kind, loving *"most wonderful mother on the planet"* for them.

And I want my last words to them be ones of love and appreciation.

As my grandmother would say, "Grazie miei amici e buon viaggio!"

Thank you, my friends, and have a wonderful journey!

Epilogue

Dolce

I've reiterated throughout this book—and I've always said and will say—my children are my and Peter's greatest creations, and I am sticking to it! They are kind, loving, generous souls who make me proud.

And so is my own mother, though it took me a long time to realize that.

My mom is ninety-six years old and lives in her home with a companion caretaker. She dresses herself every morning with matching earrings and sandals. God forbid if anyone suggest she wear a blouse that does not share a color with her pants. Mom, with encouragement, takes a shower on her own, eats healthy, and with coaxing, drinks forty to fifty ounces of water a day. She takes her vitamins and is on a low dosage of a heart and thyroid medication. Her weekly hair appointments followed by her chiropractic adjustments get her out of the house, keeping her happy and healthy.

I call my mom almost every night with a, "Buona sera, Celia, come stai?"

She replies, "Bene, et tu?" and then switches to English despite my attempts to keep her talking in Italian. She gets her way most of the time.

A feisty one, my mom tells my sisters and me that she doesn't want anyone telling her what to do. Adamantly!

"Do not tell me what to drink!" she'll say when we ask her to drink more water and not have a second glass of wine with her dinner. We have signs all over the house reminding her to drink water so her kidneys stay healthy. She makes faces and says, "Piche e beve, piche e beve!" (Italian for pee and drink.)

And God forbid we even suggest when she should wake up! If she is still in bed at noon, (her typical wakeup time), we will tiptoe into her room and quietly say, "Good morning, Mom."

She will sometimes tell us to leave her alone, or if she is in a good mood, she will ask for a few more minutes.

We promise to come back in five or ten minutes, and if she agrees, we return in the allotted time.

Sometimes she gets up. Sometimes she doesn't.

I have resigned myself to the fact that, if I am ninety-six years old and I want to sleep in, I should be allowed to without people giving me shit about it! So I usually give in to my mom and let her sleep.

Her mother, Sabaluche—yes the same "justa you watcha me!" Sabaluche who taught me to make Gavadeel—was a tyrant to her.

My mom spent most of her free time (up to the point where she got married and moved out) in the house taking orders from my grandmother. She was required to iron and starch all her brother's shirts, help her mother prepare meals, drive her shopping, work in the garden, drive Grandma to the farm to get fresh chickens, and many other chores in and around the house.

My grandmother was adamant that my mother was not allowed to go sit out on the stoop—though my grandmother later denied such, as I pointed out in my third chapter on education. As a third-generation part to that story, I was bothered for years by the incongruent behavior of my beloved grandmother.

My grandmother had some strange perceptions of life. She suppressed my mother in so many ways, telling her what to do, what to say, what to wear, who she could have as friends... And on top of it, she called my mom *stupido* while putting my dad, and all the men in her life, up on pedestals. The men could do no wrong in Sabaluche's eyes.

Yes, this is the same grandmother who I adored and idolized as a child, blissfully ignorant of this side of her.

Considering that oppressive life, I have to give my mother credit. She put up with her mother and took care of her until her last days of life. She took the good from her upbringing and was her best version of a mother to me and my siblings.

She wasn't perfect though. Certainly not perfect! And growing up, I so wished for that perfect mother that I was going to be!

When I told my mom I was writing a book on parenting, she gave me an intense questioning look and said, "I hope you are only writing good things about me!"

I took a deep breath, and without skipping a beat, I replied, "Absolutely, Mom!"

But she sensed something and gave me a stare. "Patricia?" she pressed, in that voice she uses when she is not happy with me.

I quickly changed the subject!

I spent a large part of my life not wanting to be like my mom—a lot of it was because of the terrible way my grandmother portrayed my mom to me when I was very impressionable. And God forbid you (or my husband) point out to me that I was acting or speaking like her!

Yet here I am, just starting my seventh decade and feeling compassion for her life's experience from childhood to beyond.

I want to be (and I think I am) just like her in some ways: strong, healthy, feisty, and wanting to sleep until whatever hours I choose, drink what I choose, and do whatever I choose to do. I won't feel guilty about eating ice-cream, Racioppi's Tarrelles (dunked in wine), and onion pie—

Okay, maybe I'll feel a *little* guilty.

Yet I *am* also different from her in many ways. My mom never had her own opinions. At least not that she outwardly expressed. She repeated opinions that I heard her friends tell her. She never spoke up to our father when I knew she adamantly disagreed with him. And she complained about my dad and other people behind their backs. Those three things were the most unsettling to me as a child. I heard her tell her friends stories about my dad and say she would tell him a thing or two—and then she never did.

I thought she was a coward and vowed I would not be like that. I would be bold and assertive when I had a husband! (And I am...now. Mostly always. At least in the past twenty years. Just ask Peter!)

Over time, I watched my mom's behavior shift from passive to aggressive. She completely bypassed the assertive aspect of communication. I was aware of those states because of my experience with psychotherapy.

That being said, my mom gave me a foundation that is at the core of who I am.

But it is not all that I am!

I had to find my way to navigate this world of parenting as my own person, compassionately and assertively.

My mom used to (and come to think of it, still does) tell me, "You are too nice," when I generously help people with my time, money, or energy.

But what is *too* nice? It is a phrase my mother used a lot. And I do too! Is my mom referring to me driving my grandmothers to the store, the bank, the beauty parlor…? Shoveling snow for the neighbor? Doing volunteer work at the church? Cooking meals for our extended family on holidays? I could go on with more, but suffice to say, my mom is guilty of all these "nice" things too (and more). I adopted her behavior, and then like a good daughter, passed it on to my daughter.

I remind my mother, "The apple didn't fall too far from the tree," and then say, "Grazie, Mama. Te amo." (Thank you, Mom. I love you.)

***

As my mother has aged, I've felt more compassion for her, and I have tried very consciously to see my mother through a different lens than when I was a young girl. My mom raised us four kids without much help from my father (who worked ninety hours a week), and all four of us turned out to be healthy, respectful, hardworking individuals who are passionate about the careers they chose. I see now that she helped create that. I look at her strength and vitality—she is ninety-six!—and realize she has been a good role model.

She was not perfect, and it all turned out okay.

I wish I had been able to see that in her when I was a child and had been more forgiving.

When I am with her now, I make it a point to let her know that she taught us so much: how to fix things around the house, how to have common sense and figure out solutions to challenges, how to be creative and find ways to get what you need in situations that may seem unsurmountable. And I let her know how much I love and appreciate her.

I hope it is enough to balance out all the years of blaming her for all my problems.

Are there patterns you have carried from your mother (or father or other parental figure) that are not who you want to be? It is never too late to examine those traits and change them for your actions to be in alignment with your spirit.

This book has allowed me to see how each generation does its best to foster the next generation. The more conscious we become as people, the more we work on being the best version of ourselves—and the more we are having a positive impact on humanity.

In many ways, I wrote this book for myself. I had a lot of my own shit to work through as a parent—and that I'm still learning even through the last rounds of edits. Just like I wanted to be the mother I'd wished I'd had as a child, I want to be the resource I wish I'd had as a parent. I want to share the recipe that I was *shown,* but not exactly taught. I want to share it how I wanted to receive it: broken down into simple, repeatable, manageable, and above all, *customizable* steps.

I knew all these things I wanted were inside of me, that they *did* exist. These ingredients, as basic as the carbon, hydrogen, and oxygen in our cells, were there and had been there all along. But I didn't truly *realize* the full truth of it all until I started putting in the work required to write all these truths down, to *truly* pass them on as a usable recipe.

Intuition.

Philosophy.

Unconditional Love.

They sound so simple, yet they are as infinite and complex as the space between an atom's nucleus and its circling electrons, as the grains of all the flours in all the world's Italian kitchens, and as the relationship between parents and children.

I hope this recipe helps you struggle just a little less as a parent. I hope it gives you a more intimate introduction to the inherent wisdom within you. And I hope it's something that can make you laugh with your loved ones around your busy, messy, and nourishing kitchen.

While I needed to write the book for me, I'm *sharing* it with you. My desire is you discover *your* best version of the recipe for your family. May you usher any children in your life—your own children, nieces, nephews, niblings[15] (another word I learned from my editor to avoid assuming gender), friends' children, students, whoever—into this world with a sense of empowerment while you, yourself, discover and strengthen your own inner truth.

After all, our path may not be perfect, and we may not always make the best decisions, but we must be true to ourselves.

You and your children have the answers inside of you if you just listen and trust, if you live true to your values and philosophy, and if you approach every encounter from a space of unconditional love. Your journey—and your children's journey—is to create a version of this recipe that best serves your own families.

Buon appetite!

Author Acknowledgements

This book may never have been written if not for a fateful lunch in Phoenix, Arizona with our friends and colleagues, Brandy and Don MacDonald in February almost twenty years before publishing this book. They asked me what my next big adventure would be now that I was semiretired from my practice. I said that I had been thinking about (and telling friends, colleagues, and family) for the prior fifteen years that I was going to write a book on parenting. Brandy stated that her husband had also been planning to write a book, and she'd finally gotten sick of hearing him just talk about it, so she'd said, "shit or get off the pot" and make it happen. She connected him with a writing angel in Australia, Clare McIvor, who had written books with other chiropractors, and six months later, his book was completed.

My husband had been listening and asked Don for this writing angel's contact info, and within ten minutes, I had an appointment to speak to Clare. I think Peter was feeling like Brandy, but too kind to tell me to "shit or get off the pot." So, he did the next best thing.

I have been through a few editors since Clare McIvor helped me write the book. Claire gave me the confidence to conceive of and then vomit the book out of me (sort of like the first few months of both of my pregnancies). Thank you so much Claire. Thank you, Mary Elizabeth Wheeler and James Sanguinetti, for your insights. And many thanks to my whimsical, fairy-godmother editor, Trisha Wooldridge, for being the last person to help "push" this proverbial baby out of me.

I also want to thank Nic LaRue for being my website guru, helping me launch my author website, and teaching me how to best use it; Kristi Petersen Schoonover for designing and printing my antipasto chap book; Rich Storrs for being our fantastic closing editor; and last but not least, Angi Shearstone for not one, but *two* gorgeous covers (for the chap book and this book), and doing the interior layout and design.

Here we are, years after the fateful lunch and subsequent first meeting with my editor/writing angel. My long-awaited book is here for the reading. I did print a "chap book" in December of 2023 as a tasty morsel of what was yet to come. I needed a product to keep me motivated while I continued what became an arduous task to complete the book in my version of Perfect.

I have had many angels surrounding me during this labor of love. I look at this experience similar to my pregnancy and subsequent labor and delivery. I just birthed my fourth child! My practice being my first baby, and then Katie and Christopher. Throughout all these creations, my biggest cheerleader and coach has been my husband, Peter Kevorkian. He has continued to encourage me in all aspects of my life to be the shining light that he knows me to be. I am still trying to believe I am the person he sees in me. He is my best friend, my amazing partner in our practice and marriage of over forty years, and the best father/co-parent to my children I could ever have dreamed for.

This book would absolutely not be possible if not for our children, Katie and Christopher. They are our greatest creation and have been our "experiments in the making" (as all children are) as you have read in these pages. They reflect back to me the kindness, respect and enthusiasm for life that Peter and I took great care in modeling for them. When Katie was born, I was so full of love for her that I didn't think there would be enough for any more children. When Christopher was born, I realized that there are no bounds to love. The more I loved, the more there was available for all I touched in all aspects of my life.

When our children were born, our chiropractic family practice grew in leaps and bounds as we attracted pregnant women, their partners, and their newborn babies to begin a journey of health and wellness with us as their guides. I have gleaned so much from all our patients, especially our platinum members, some of whom have been with us from before our children were born. They are like family and I need to include them and hundreds of other patients in this acknowledgement.

I am blessed to have two amazing parents, Cecelia (Carola) Giuliano, alive and well in her mid-nineties and Armando Giuliano (who passed in November, 2019). They instilled in me and my siblings an ethic to be thoughtful, respectful, and helpful (to a fault) in all our interactions with people. I would not be the person I am today if not for them.

To my siblings, Armand, Terry, and Linda, thank you for growing up with me and putting up with me. We are proof that even with the same parents our life purpose and personalities come in with us at birth and are expressed uniquely. We each found success in our lives by emulating the foundational principles and ethics instilled in us by our parents.

My grandmothers, Isabella (Laterza) Carola (aka Sabaluche) and Vincenza (Mascellino) Giuliano (aka grandma Jenny), were a powerful force in our families and especially in my life. Their personalities were polar opposites, and they clashed most of the time, but they each expressed their love for their families using food as their medium. They were great role models for me.

I must also thank DD Palmer for discovering chiropractic and shedding a new philosophy of life and living to the world. And to his son, BJ Palmer who founded the first chiropractic college in Davenport, Iowa and expanded on the philosophy of life that governs my life and that of my family.

Finally, so many thanks to my friends, my colleagues, and relatives who encouraged me to "hurry up and write this book! I need help now!" Your enthusiasm supported me in this labor of love beyond what words can say. I can't even begin to name all of you, but know I love you all!

The philosophy of life expounded upon in this book is not particular to chiropractors alone; it is a philosophy of life and living that acknowledges that "life expresses intelligence"—(Thank you, Dr. Jeannie Ohm, for that perfect wording and for being my friend and mentor.)—a truth so profound and so simple as not to be accepted by many.

Once again, thank you all. I love and appreciate you!

About the Author

Dr. Patricia A. Giuliano has been a leading light and voice in the chiropractic and natural health communities for over forty years. While she steadfastly declares her children, Katie and Christopher, are the greatest creations from her and her husband, "Dr. Patti" has "mothered" and "parented" many great things into the world, starting with Back Bay Chiropractic, her first office, and then Westwood Family Chiropractic, which she began in 1984 with her husband, Dr. Peter Kevorkian, and which has become one of the largest-family centered chiropractic offices in the world, serving people of all ages from newborns to seniors.

A founding member and former president of the League of Chiropractic Women, Dr. Patti's influence has been essential in increasing the percentage of women speaking on chiropractic stages. Her clinical and educational ventures have helped expand chiropractic care and awareness into the realms of the pre-natal, pregnancy, and chiropractic pediatric population, ultimately increasing the availability of chiropractic care to more women, infants, children—and their families. She and Dr. Peter have housed and mentored over forty interns, as these students completed their final three months of clinical and educational requirements for graduation.

Her greatest passion is to connect with people and make a difference in their lives. Whether speaking one-on-one with patients and clients or addressing a room of hundreds during one of her many inspirational speaking engagements, Dr. Patti is a gifted and intuitive storyteller who seeks to heal and empower as many people as she can, and to expand the minds and hearts of all she touches.

Besides her personal and professional accomplishments, she has been honored by several prestigious awards, including the

Lighthouse Award and Chiropractor of the Year in Massachusetts; Regent of the Year and Chiropractor of the Year at Sherman College of Chiropractic; Philosophy of Chiropractic award from the New Beginnings seminars; the League of Chiropractic Women's Legacy Award; and the Dr. Irene Gold Philosophy of Chiropractic Award. Dr. Patti has also been a noted speaker and guest lecturer at colleges and universities all over the world.

Finally, Dr. Patti is an excellent cook, practitioner of beach therapy, and giver of hugs.

Find out more about Dr. Patti at DrPattiGiuliano.com.

About the Editor

Trisha J. Wooldridge (child-friendly T.J. Wooldridge) is an award-winning pan-genre, pan-media chaos word witch. She's edited over four hundred books, including the NYT-bestselling *Cross* by D.A. Roach, the award-winning *The Underground* by Roxanne Bland, and books by NYT bestselling author Kelly Hashway. She has acquired fiction for a mid-size press, freelanced for several small presses, edited eight anthologies, and curated three more. While most of her work has been in speculative fiction (horror, fantasy, and science fiction), she's also worked on non-fiction titles in business, food, psychology, and spirituality. She's also edited the writing for the MMORPG *Dungeons & Dragons: Stormreach*, composed multiple study guides for *Frankenstein; or the Modern Prometheus*, and developed over a dozen online writing and publishing courses for the New England Horror Writers.

While she loves editing, Trisha's main passion is writing. Find her work in the Shirley Jackson Award-winning *The Twisted Book of Shadows*; some *HWA Poetry Showcase* volumes; all of the New England Horror Writer anthologies (that she didn't edit); *Don't Turn Out the Lights: A Tribute to Alvin Schwartz's Scary Stories to Tell in the Dark*; *Pseudopod* podcast; and *34 Orchard* literary journal. CKP/New Mythology Press publishes her fantasy series, "The 27 Kingdoms," and her first fiction-poetry collection, *Where Monsters Pray,* was released June 2024 from Pink Narcissus Press.

Her prior work includes interviewing Goth and Metal bands; selling wine; reviewing restaurants; writing for food industry magazines; and coordinating events and PR for Annie's Book Stop of Worcester, MA.

Former president of Broad Universe, an organization promoting and supporting women and underrepresented voices in writing, Trisha now serves on the New England Horror Writers board and is an active member of HWA and SFPA. She spends rare moments of mystical "free time" with a very patient Husband-of-Awesome; a tiny witch kitty; a large witcher kitty; a rescued bay gelding; and a matronly calico mare.

Find out more about Trish at www.anovelfriend.com.

Notes

1. The Apgar score, developed by Virgina Apgar, MD, is a test performed on newborns within 1-5 minutes before birth that determines how the baby tolerated birthing. On a 1-10 scale the higher the number the better the immediate health. A score of under 7 usually signifies the need for medical attention. The score is not meant to predict the child's future health. "APGAR Score." National Library of Medicine. www.ncbi.nlm.nih.gov/books/NBK470569

2. Frederick Leboyer was a French obstetrician who wrote the groundbreaking book, *Birth Without Violence,* in 1975, which gives poetic descriptions of potential perceptions and feelings of embryos, fetuses, and newborns. His work started the movement of gentler birthing methods, paving the way for the practice of water birth and unassisted childbirth.

3. Published in 1976, the original *Spiritual Midwifery* by Ina May Gaskin, breathed new life into the all-but-vanished field of midwifery and introduced an new generation to the possibility of home birth and breast feeding. The book is currently in its fourth edition.

4. Louise Lynn Hay was an American motivational author, professional speaker, and AIDS advocate. She authored several self-help books, including the 1984 title, *You Can Heal Your Life,* and founded Hay House publishing. www.louisehay.com

5. Founded over a century ago by Dr. Maria Montessori, an Italian physician, the child-focused Montessori Method has transformed schools worldwide by fostering a rigorous, self-motivated approach to educating children and adolescents in cognitive, emotional, social, and physical growth and development. American Montessori Society. amshq.org/About-Montessori/What-Is-Montessori

6. The Spellers Method™ is a multidisciplinary educational model, curriculum, and mentorship program to help nonspeakers across a variety of sensory-motor profiles who spell or type to communicate. spellers.com/about-spellers-method

7. This is Trisha's personal summary, but she highly suggests you also read Dani Rodwell's much more detailed article, "Neurospicy Meaning: What it Means and Where it Came From," at NeurosparkHealth.com. www.neurosparkhealth.com/blog/neurospicy-meaning-what-it-means-and-where-it-came-from.html

8. Hallowell, Edward, MD, and John Ratey, MD. "ADHD needs a better name. We have one." ADDitudemag.com www.additudemag.com/attention-deficit-disorder-vast

9. Olivardia, Roberto, PhD. "Is your ADHD Brain Hard-Wired for Obesity?" ADDitudeMag.com. www.additudemag.com/adhd-and-obesity-hard-wired-for-weight-gain

10. The Hoffman Quadrinity Process®, founded by Bob Hoffman in 1967, is taught through a week-long residential and personal growth retreat that helps participants identify negative behaviors, moods, and ways of thinking that developed unconsciously and were conditioned in childhood. Hoffman Institute. www.hoffmaninstitute.org/the-process

11. Ram Dass, also known as Baba Ram Dass, was an American spiritual teacher, guru of modern yoga, psychologist, and writer. His best-selling 1971 book *Be Here Now*, which has been described by multiple reviewers as "seminal", helped popularize Eastern spirituality and yoga in the West. www.ramdass.org

12. LSD was illegal and pooh-poohed in the sixties by the establishment and is now being used in therapeutic settings to help people with depression and PTSD. "FDA Opens the Door to Clinical Use of LSD." www.webmd.com/mental-health/news/20240326/fda-opens-the-door-clinical-use-lsd

13. Patti's family used Care.com and interviewed people, but check online, with doctors, at various community centers, through libraries, and more to find what works best for you.

14. Lasix, or furosemide, is a common diuretic prescribed to people with congestive heart failure and kidney issues. www.drugs.com/lasix.html

15. "Nibling" is a gender-neutral term used to refer to a child of one's sibling as a replacement for "niece" or "nephew." The word is thought to have been coined in the early 1950s, but was relatively obscure for several decades before being revived in recent years. www.merriam-webster.com/wordplay/words-were-watching-nibling

Further References and Resources

Some of these resources are specific to the U.S., but I (Patti) don't feel comfortable making suggestions outside of resources I've personally used or heard good things about. For readers outside of the U.S., you may find more useful resources through your local communities, libraries, medical facilities, and schools.

Birthing Process

Leboyer, Frederick. *Birth without Violence.* New York: Simon & Schuster, 1974.

Ohm, Jeanne, DC. "Birthing with the Wisdom of the Ages." Pathways to Family Wellness. pathwaystofamilywellness.org/chiropractic/birthing-with-the-wisdom-of-the-ages.html

Ray, Sondra. *Ideal Birth.* Berkeley, CA: Celestial Arts, 1985.

Romeo, Catherine, and Claudia Panuthos. *Ended Beginnings: Healing Childbearing Losses.* Westport, CT: Praeger, 1984.

Sidenbladh, Erik. *Water Babies: A Book About Igor Tjarkovsky and His Method for Delivering and Training.* New York: St. Martin's Press, 1983.

Breastfeeding

"Breastfeeding." Centers for Disease Control. www.cdc.gov/nutrition/infantandtoddlernutrition/breastfeeding/ recommendations-benefits.html

Global Breastfeeding Collective. www.globalbreastfeedingcollective.org

La Leche League International. *llli.org*

"Mastitis." The Mayo Clinic. www.mayoclinic.org/diseases-conditions/mastitis/ symptoms-causes/syc-20374829

Child Development

Pearce, Joseph Chilton. *Magical Child.* Barrington, IL: Rocking Horse Books, 1977.

Chiropractic

Academy of Chiropractic Family Practice. chiropracticfamilypractice.org

International Chiropractic Pediatric Association. icpa4kids.com

League of Chiropractic Women. www.lcwomen.com

Life West Chiropractic College. lifewest.edu

Oklahaven Children's Chiropractic Center. chiropractic4kids.com

"The Palmer Family." Palmer College of Chiropractic. www.palmer.edu/about-palmer/palmer-college-history/the-palmer-family

Pathways to Family Wellness Magazine. pathwaystofamilywellness.org

Stephenson, R. W. D.C., Ph.C. *Chiropractic Textbook.* Davenport, IA: Palmer School of Chiropractic, 1927.

Westwood Family Chiropractic. www.westwoodfamilychiropractic.com

Death Planning

Gawande, Atul. *Being Mortal.* New York, NY: Picador, 2017.

*Oh Fu@k, I'm Dead! Now What? *Important Sh*t You Need to Know When I Die.** Peace of Mind and Heart Planners. 2021.

Order of the Good Death. www.orderofthegooddeath.com

Education

American Montessori Society. amshq.org/About-Montessori/What-Is-Montessori

Applied Scholastics. www.appliedscholastics.org/schools-programs.html

Delphi Academy of Boston. delphiboston.org

Delphian School, The. www.delphian.org

Spellers Freedom Foundation. spellers.com/about-spellers-method

Sudbury Valley School. https://sudburyvalley.org

Elder Care

Care.com. https://www.care.com

Meal Train. https://www.mealtrain.com

Visiting Angels. https://www.visitingangels.com

Midwifery

Gaskin, Ina May, and The Farm. *Spiritual Midwifery.* Summertown, TN: Book Publishing Company, 1975.

Neurodiverse Topics

ADDitude. www.additudemag.com

Meara, Killian. "FDA Grants Breakthrough Therapy Designation to LSD-Based Treatment for Generalized Anxiety Disorder." Drug Topics. www.drugtopics.com/view/fda-grants-breakthrough-therapy-designation-to-lsd-based-treatment-for-generalized-anxiety-disorder

Olivardia, Roberto. "Is your ADHD Brain Hard-Wired for Obesity?" *ADDitudeMag.com.* https://www.additudemag.com/adhd-and-obesity-hard-wired-for-weight-gain

Rodwell, Dani. "Neurospicy Meaning: What it Means and Where it Came From." NeuroSpark Health. www.neurosparkhealth.com/blog/neurospicy-meaning-what-it-means-and-where-it-came-from.html

Terry, Ken. "FDA Opens the Door to Clinical Use of LSD." WebMD. www.webmd.com/mental-health/news/20240326/fda-opens-the-door-clinical-use-lsd

Persons Referenced in Book

Braden, Gregg. greggbraden.com

Brown, Brené. Brenébrown.com

Campion, Lisa. lisacampion.com

Cayce, Edgar. www.edgarcayce.org

Choquette, Sonia. soniachoquette.net

Davis, Adelle. www.adelledavis.org

Hay, Louise. www.louisehay.com

Prenatal Care and Research

Kurtzman, Laura. "Study Finds Wide Exposure to Environmental Toxics in Cohort of Pregnant Women." ObGyn&RS Maternal-Fetal Medicine & Reproductive Genetics. obgyn.ucsf.edu/news/toxic-chemicals-pregnant-women-and-their-newborns

Street, Mary Elizabeth, and Sergio Bernasconi. "Endocrine-Disrupting Chemicals in Human Fetal Growth." National Library of Medicine. www.ncbi.nlm.nih.gov/pmc/articles/PMC7073082

Wellness and Spirituality

Active Healing. www.activehealing.org

Dass, Ram. *Be Here Now.* New York, NY: Harmony, 1971.

Hoffman Institute. www.hoffmaninstitute.org

Institutes for the Achievement of Human Potential. iahp.org

Williamson, Marianne. *A Return to Love: Reflections on the Principles of "A Course in Miracles".* New York, NY: HarperOne, 1996.

* 9 7 9 8 2 2 7 6 0 5 0 0 9 *